EVERYTHING A BAND-AID CAN'T FIX

A TEEN'S GUIDE TO HEALING AND DEALING WITH LIFE

NICOLE RUSSELL

WISE
CREATIVE + PUBLISHING
Ink
2012

ISBN 13: 978-1-63489-147-9

Library of Congress Catalog Number: 2018950383
Printed in the United States of America
First Printing: 2018
23   22   21   20   19   9   8   7   6

Cover design by Liz Casal
Interior design by Kim Morehead
Illustrations by Fabio Mancini

Wise Ink Creative Publishing
807 Broadway St. NE, Suite 46
Minneapolis, MN 55413
wiseink.com

To order, visit itascabooks.com or call 1-800-901-3480. Reseller discounts available.

I dedicate this book to my dad. Thank you for being present and for all of your sacrifices.

To my mom, who instilled all of the values in me that I carry today.

To every guest speaker, friend, board member, and volunteer who has given their time and support to the youth of Precious Dreams Foundation.

To KJ, Zoe, Steele, Sage, Cori, Bronx, London, Romeo, River, and Andre.

Most importantly, I dedicate this book to the best thing that ever happened to me: my little sister, my star, Miracle (and to her family, for allowing us to continue our sisterhood even after she went back to live with them).

Table of Contents

Dear _____,

People with capes and magical powers don't exist in this world. Starting right now, I want you to forget everything you've been shown about dependency and discover your ability to save yourself. You may have your own way of handling life, but I want you to be open to trying something new. This is for your benefit, not mine.

Next time you wake up from a nightmare, stay in bed and reflect on what just occurred and how it made you feel. Stay in the fearful thoughts for a minute and analyze them. What did you see, think, or feel that inspired the night terror? Going forward, share it. Could you have reacted differently to any of the things that occurred? Being in a negative headspace is not a bad thing— ignoring it is!

When you have a good dream you want to share it with the world, but when it's a bad one, you try to block it out of your memory. Going forward, face it all. I want you to spend time dealing with everything and sharing the good and the bad. Things that we don't care for don't get fixed, and whatever you cover still exists.

Healing processes look different in every scenario, but one thing remains true in all situations, even with a physical wound—you must tend to it before you can expect it to heal.

This book was written for YOU and all the curious young adults who are looking for an instruction manual on how to deal with the craziness of the teen years. It's a set of guidelines for understanding how to cope with feelings and experiences that aren't always easy to share. It will help you master the ability to defeat adversity with or without the help of others; it will encourage you to speak out against the wrongs in your world and help you protect yourself from them.

Normal is dealing with peer pressure, health issues, bullying, breakups, failure, vile thoughts, a broken home, unstable friendships, and simply being different. Normal is having to comfort yourself when everything goes wrong and life sucks. Normal is a choice. As a teen, you have no way of avoiding what you're unprepared to face—the challenge lies in how you react to things that happen to you and whether you choose to heal or deal with them.

This book will take you on a journey of self-care that you can use for the rest of your life. Let's take the first step together.

Preface

"When I grow up, I just want to be a man. A man who can provide for his family." Those thoughts alone are what kept seventeen-year-old Justin focused on his goals when he was living in an NYC homeless shelter with his mother and sister.

Serving as the cofounder and executive director of Precious Dreams Foundation has provided me with many opportunities to supply comfort to thousands of at-risk youth like Justin. Along the way, conversations with participants have left me with eye-opening and sometimes heartbreaking examples of how truly difficult the journey can be for each unique individual. As a result of my encounters with underserved youth, I've come to believe that the most beautiful, inspiring stories belong to people who've fought the toughest battles and overcome adversity on their own; these are the admirable humans who envisioned a future unlike their reality and held tight to the possibilities of tomorrow.

This book was inspired by people who understand that where they started is far from where they will finish and who know that they're fully capable of achieving greatness. These people have faced countless forms of adversity and unimaginable hardships. By listening to their stories, I've come to realize how truly important it is to work on yourself in order to persevere.

Their personal traumas motivated me to create a program through Precious Dreams Foundation entitled "Comfort Drop," which focuses on providing experiences that inspire and teach transitional youth how to find comfort within. The program has enabled me to introduce guest speakers who share personal stories of overcoming obstacles with thousands of teens in New York, South Florida, Baltimore, and California. Many of the guest speakers are celebrities or friends of mine; they're people I cherish, and you'll find quotes from their contributions to Precious Dreams Foundation throughout this book. I've learned from my conversations with our unique guest speakers that they all have one thing in common: they started envisioning their best life during their childhood.

I firmly believe that if people learn to self-comfort at an early age, they'll have an advantage in achieving contentment. I know many adults who are still fighting to control the negative thoughts in their heads. Some of these people experienced trauma in their childhoods and have grown up to repeat the cycle—never letting go of pain, holding themselves prisoner to bitterness and self-victimization, and not allowing themselves to heal from their past. The older you get, the harder it becomes to outgrow unhealthy habits of thinking.

I created this book to give young adults a jump-start at discovering the most important tool needed to face life's uncertainties: themselves. My hope is that teens will find inspiration from people who didn't have many resources but still wrote their best stories. I hope that those who read these chapters will find the strength they need to overcome obstacles, persevere, and replace sadness or anger with determination.

CHAPTER 1

Self-Comfort 101

"I call it the funk [depression]. I lost my grandma at age nine, my cousin Terrence one year, and my father died three days before my fifteenth birthday. I don't think I ever learned how to cope with it properly, but anxiety and depression all have a way of creeping up on you. I was in a deep depression for what felt like forever but was actually a few months. The things that got me out of it were thinking positive, talking to family, reading self-help books, and exercise. I slowly found myself enjoying things again and then one day I realized I wasn't depressed anymore."

—A$AP Ferg, rapper, songwriter, and designer

If an adult purchased or recommended this book for you, you're most likely thinking: *To self-comfort is to comfort yourself. Got it. It's pretty self-explanatory, and I'd rather skip through and read the quotes.* Wait—this book is so much more, and I promise you won't regret reading it in its entirety. But you can read it out of order, flip through the pages, or take it from start to finish; there are no rules here. Take notes, underline areas, or take pictures of quotes and share them with friends. Use this as a guide and an inspiration to help you help yourself.

Learning to comfort yourself is not just a survival tactic; it promotes a healthier way to live. At some point, almost every adult will consciously make an effort to find inner peace and learn how to self-soothe. This self-preservation goes beyond simply overcoming stress—it's a state of mind. Most adults would say their journey to self-care and self-awareness began in their mid to late twenties and is something they still struggle with. I know I still do. It was only through experience that I learned life goes on, things get better, sometimes I'll only have myself to depend on, and that's okay.

This book not only gives you an advantage in life but also provides the tools for self-comfort when they're most beneficial: your teenage years. Let's start with the basics.

#SelfComfort

What Is Self-Comfort?
Self-comfort is the ability to calm oneself when dealing with stressful situations, frustrations, or sadness. It is how you successfully face and work through problems on your own. It is honoring needs that lead to helpful outcomes. Having the ability to self-comfort does not mean you don't need help from others. However, it's a liberating way to self-sufficiently build resilience so you can bounce back from hard times and avoid making situations worse.

Self-comforters (yes, I made that word up) are like superheroes: they're unstoppable, they're unbreakable, and they understand that being "unbothered" is really just dealing with being bothered in a healthy way. Self-comforters realize that they don't need to be saved by anybody else because they are their own solution.

Once you learn how to self-comfort, there's absolutely nothing you can't overcome, no matter where you live, who your family is, what you lack, or how difficult your situation may be. The first step to self-comfort is believing that you can and discovering your mental strength.

How would you rate your mental strength in this present moment on a scale of 1–5? (Circle one.)

1   I feel weak most days

2   I'm surviving

3   I know what's best for me, although I don't always follow my own advice

4   I'm strong enough

5   I'm fully aware of myself and my needs, and my priority is to remain in good health

We all practice self-soothing techniques on a regular basis without realizing it. You may not be a master, but here are a couple examples of how you're already ahead in the self-comforting game:

Have you ever realized, when you stub your toe or bump your head, you grab tightly onto the place of pain and rub or squeeze it until it feels better? You don't wait for someone else to rub it before you unconsciously try to comfort yourself. (Plus, that would be pretty weird . . . having someone else rub your toe.)

When faced with an intolerable situation, you might find an empty room to release your angst or create distance to be alone with your thoughts. Choosing an environment that doesn't fuel your frustrations is the first step in calming yourself down.

Mastering the ability to self-comfort might feel like one of the hardest things to do because we're surrounded by forms of dependency in our relationships, government, and living environments. We're taught to "cry on a shoulder," but tears naturally fall on our own faces, and there's nothing wrong with them landing there. It may feel more comforting to cry to others, but it should never feel bad to cry alone. We're taught to look outward for answers when we fall short. Looking outward to people who have your best interest in mind isn't a bad thing, but relying on them to always be there is.

Many difficult situations would benefit from the use of self-comforting techniques. At your age, your stress may stem from any of the following:

- Pressure to perform well in school

- Self-image
- Dealing with sexual feelings
- Relationship drama
- Family issues
- Peer pressure
- Financial concerns
- Being unsure of your future
- Worrying about the safety of loved ones
- Feeling like you don't have control over your life
- Parental expectations
- Being misunderstood
- Cyberbullying

Learning healthy ways to cope with these issues has copious benefits. Self-comforting encourages problem-solving rather than avoidance and provides strategies to live a more fruitful life. Since you're here, gift yourself the happiness you deserve.

People who are depressed often use less skillful approaches to solving their problems than those who self-comfort. They might end up attaching themselves to others, avoiding the issues, or overindulging in unhealthy activities, food, drugs, or alcohol. Sometimes these things feel like fun distractions, but they can end up creating bigger issues. If you know something is bad for you but do it anyway, you're ignoring the root of the problem.

The original mission of my nonprofit, Precious Dreams Foundation, was to provide bags filled with bedside comfort items such as pajamas, plush toys, journals, books, blankets, stress balls, and other miscellaneous tools that enable kids to relax, rest peacefully, and forget about their worries. These simple items provide a sense of security and self-confidence and can be used as an outlet or distraction to pull attention away from negative thoughts. Healthy comfort items interfere with the mind's desire to be reactive to whatever is throwing it off balance, and incorporating them at a young age is helpful.

People use different methods to help themselves cope, but even adults use comfort items. In a 2012 poll, Travelodge discovered that 35 percent of adults in Britain still sleep with teddy bears or comparable plush items. Another popular comfort tool is a book—focusing on the words of a good novel helps to clear your mind. According to a study conducted by the University of Sussex in the United Kingdom, reading for just six minutes can reduce your stress levels by as much as 68 percent.

When you're acting alone but using a positive tool, it is still considered self-comfort. Take pride in your comfort tools, enjoy them, and keep them safe. However, never become completely attached to or overly reliant on these objects. Comfort items get lost or stolen every day—I know I've had to deal with a lost bear or two. It can feel like a real tragedy, but if you lose a comfort item, don't panic. Trust me, you'll find another.

What gives you comfort and why? (It could be a person, place, or thing.)

_____

_____

_____

How would you feel if the thing that gives you comfort were taken away?
Can you comfort yourself without it?

_____

_____

_____

_____

Do you have any unhealthy habits for feeling good?

_____

_____

_____

_____

What natural skill do you have that assists you in finding comfort during
hard times? For example: an artistic skill can help take your mind off of
your current situation. Dancing helps me self-comfort.

_____

_____

Once you can identify positive strategies and comfort tools, you gain confidence in your ability to deal with discomfort.

Chapter 1
Remedies and Takeaways:

- Self-comfort saves lives.

- As a teen, you are living in either the best or the worst time of your life. The experiences, whether good or bad, will all pass, so enjoy them or be patient with them.

- Honor your needs that lead to healthy outcomes.

- In order to identify the best way to self-comfort, recognize the positive options you currently have or depend on for solace.

- It's unhealthy to completely rely on a comfort option that can be taken away.

- Begin to recognize how you can comfort yourself without the help of others.

CHAPTER 2

Perfect Family, Anyone?

I was thankful for my mom, but wondered why I had to be adopted. Why I couldn't just be raised by the mother who birthed me like everyone else? I was born during a civil war in El Salvador, to my birth mother, who wasn't able to care for me, and I was raised by my most wonderful mother who adopted me when I was a baby. It took me a long time to speak those words out loud, and even longer to truly accept who I am, my multiple identities that don't fit into a box. But the truth is, there is no blueprint for normal, or family.

—Sadye Campoamor,
director of community affairs, NYCDOE

I've always had a rebellious yet ethical style. At age six, my parents' relationship had been on and off for, well, most of my life. My mom and dad were always fighting over infidelity and typical parental disagreements, even though I remember my mother trying to hide her sadness behind smiles of admiration for my brother and me. My parents had a really bad argument one night, and I became a witness to domestic violence for the first time in my life. Violence was never a topic in our home, but I instinctively knew it was wrong. Immediately following the physical encounter, my mother left our home, only to find herself coming back and sleeping on the floor of my room at night.

At age six, sharing a room with my mother was the best sleepover I could ask for, but I knew she was sleeping there because she and my father were not getting along. I didn't understand why my mother preferred to sleep in the house, but selfishly, I appreciated the time we shared. We stayed up late having girl talk, and she let me play with her hair. I loved every second of it, but my feelings of excitement over our sleeping arrangements were short-lived. I sensed that my mother was trying to mask her pain, and I wanted to help her help herself.

I remember telling her that she should leave because I wanted her to be happy. I didn't *really* want my mother to move out of the house, but I loved her deeply and could feel her pain every time I looked into her eyes. I felt everything my mother felt, and as much as I wanted both parents in my home, I didn't think it was fair for them to suffer and sacrifice their happiness for mine. As an adult, I now see that parents sacrificing their happiness for the sake of their children is common in many households . . . and sometimes the kids grow up having no idea.

Shortly after our conversation, my mother left. I felt lost. I was embarrassed and didn't want any of my peers to know I was a victim of a broken family. Dealing with my own emotions on top of the new changes to our household routine was difficult, but missing my mother was the hardest part. I was struggling to deal with her absence in my own head, and I had difficulty articulating my inner turmoil to others.

#DivorceHasNothingToDoWithTheKids

To cope, I focused on the idea that my mother could start a new journey and be happy. It seemed unfair to me, but I had to remember she was not only my mother but also a person who deserved a happy life. I also knew that just because I didn't live with my mother didn't mean I didn't have one. When I found myself focusing on the negative aspects of the situation or dwelling on the drastic change their separation meant for my brother and me, I would remember how much better off my parents were apart. I focused on making my new life work for me. It was my way of comforting myself.

I owe a lot of my strength to my mother and to the fact that I grew up with a single dad and a big brother. The absence of my mother in our home caused my father to battle depression, although he would never admit it and was never diagnosed. It might've been the hardest thing he ever had to deal with

The only sound on any given day in our home was music. My father and I didn't communicate much. Although I tried, I was often shushed away. I remember coming home from school sometimes, saying, "Hi, Dad," and getting no response or reaction. It was as if I were living with a ghost. I cried so many days because of how much I hated my living situation. My father was miserable because of the separation, and he subconsciously took it out on us.

Parents
aren't perfect.
They are people.

I also didn't have a great relationship with my older brother, Wally. I think it had a lot to do with our astrological sign differences, but he'd say it's because I'm hardheaded. He was always bossing me around and never let me within ten feet of the fun or his friends. Our personalities were both very strong—everything I said or did seemed to annoy him. I was told that siblings were supposed to look out for one another, but my brother had his own things to worry about.

I always wished for another sibling, but I didn't get one until I was in my twenties. (Reflecting, I'd say my foster sister was totally worth the wait! Now she's a teenager and my best friend.)

My brother was so consumed with his hobbies that he didn't have time to entertain his kid sister. Wally stayed in his room with the door closed, and my father was usually fixing something while blasting music. To keep myself busy, I developed an obsession with entertaining myself in front of the mirror, singing and dancing along to the distant sound of my father's music when nobody could see or hear me. Subconsciously, I was becoming a loner.

I felt invisible most days, but the lack of attention I received forced me to see myself more deeply.

Though it's healthy to develop an understanding of yourself, it's *not* healthy to shut yourself off from others completely. We all have a profound yearning to be loved, and I believe we can often find that love in our families, despite our differences. Home is where we're taught to love, even if it isn't always easy. You're born into this world with relatives you cannot choose, incompatible siblings, or family members that have different opinions, values, and personalities. Sharing experiences with people that have opposing opinions will teach you the greatest lessons of love.

A healthy family environment provides: inclusion, food, shelter, respect, esteem, recreation, understanding, and love.

Dysfunctional Family, Anyone?
Kids accept the fact that people aren't perfect, yet they expect their family members to be.

No matter how much we'd like a perfect family, there really is no such thing. Typical dysfunction can even be found in the homes of children living with both their parents. Every family has its issues, and at some point the relationships between each individual will be tested. Some children fail to realize how blessed they are just to simply have a guardian who plays an active role in their lives. According to the US Census Bureau, in 2016, 69 percent of people under eighteen lived with two married parents, leaving the rest of the population to be raised by single parents or relatives.

Home should be a safe place, but unfortunately that's not always the case. Teens are often too embarrassed to tell others that they're living in a dysfunctional family environment. When your biggest headaches and pains come from those closest to you, you might feel like you have no escape in the world. This is frustrating, but it's not your fault. Use your comfort tools to keep your cool and protect your peace, but also be sure to listen to your gut and recognize if anything really wrong is happening.

Family members don't have a right to hurt or neglect you. If a family member makes you feel unsafe, talk to a trusted adult or professional about it. Just remember—if you share what's happening, you have to be completely honest. Never exaggerate or downplay your experiences.

Everyone, including you, deserves to be content. For parents, that might mean living outside the home in order to find themselves or discover what makes them happy.

Sometimes that's the best scenario, especially if your parents don't get along. Your parents can't love you in the best ways if they don't know how to take care of their own needs.

Your parents and relatives aren't perfect. They don't always know how best to love each other or to love you, but guess what? They're only human. You may not always agree with their choices, but they're usually trying to do their very best. While you may not understand some of their decisions right now, things may make sense to you over time.

What is your definition of family?

_____

_____

_____

_____

How are you similar to people in your immediate family?

_____

_____

_____

In what ways are you different from your family?

_____

_____

_____

List some friends or people who care about you that you consider to be as close as family.

_____

_____

_____

_____

Understand that everything a person (parent, guardian, or anyone) does is ultimately a reflection of themselves—not you! If your parents aren't present, that's because of their own issues. The only thing you can do is be grateful for the fact that you were created and have the power to achieve greatness (with or without a perfect family). Make each day count and make the most of living in a place you can't control.

Skip to Chapter 6 if this resonates with you.

Chapter 2
Remedies and Takeaways:

- Your parents won't always love you the way you want to be loved.

- Home is where all the crazy people reside.

- Don't stress over things or relationships you cannot control.

- Allow your parents the freedom to find happiness outside their relationship with you.

- Appreciate the similarities and differences between you and your family members. You were not created to be just like them.

- Find comfort in the chaos—take mental notes or write out your experiences in a journal, so you don't forget this chapter of your story.

CHAPTER 3

#AllThoughtsMatter

"Be careful what you think, because your mind is creative."
—Brandy, actress, singer, and Broadway star

Brandy shared this message with 50 teens from NYC homeless shelters at a Precious Dreams Foundation Comfort Drop, and it resonated with everyone. Your mind is where manifestation begins. How can you self soothe if your thoughts are not aligned with what you want for yourself?

#ThinkSmart

We all have an inner voice. Some are louder than others.

Your inner voice is the one reading this book to you. Do you hear it? This voice speaks only to you; it daydreams, complains, evaluates, comments, and plans for you. It even interrupts itself. It's always there, unless you learn to silence it—which is part of learning to self-comfort—and it's either working in your favor or trying to kill your joy.

The inner voice can take a bad situation and make it worse. Some of us are masters at creating destructive thoughts. While it's natural to focus on your inner voice when it's being critical, it takes strength and determination to prioritize affirming and validating ideas. Troubled thoughts often come in the form of anxiety, your brain trying to protect you from things that may not actually be a threat. Anxiety and worrisome thoughts can inspire skin picking, nail biting, hair pulling, eraser eating . . . I've seen it all. They're all natural reactions to calm ourselves.

If you're focused on the possibilities of bad grades, failing relationships, or not getting into the college of your dreams, it's more likely that those fears will come to fruition. The time you take to worry about failing the test is distracting you from focusing on passing. You'll end up running out of time, and those fears will be made manifest. You must learn how to produce the results you desire by focusing on your goals, and that starts with your thoughts.

When was the last time you apologized to yourself for the bad things you've said?

One of the best ways to calm the mind is to pick up a good book, even for just a few minutes. Breathe, read, and transport yourself to another place and time. There is literature about every topic under the sun; if you find yourself uninterested in a particular genre, perhaps you'd enjoy picking out a different book more in line with your interests.

Your inner voice determines whether you have a good or bad day. It is where peace starts and hope perseveres. It decides how hard you will work. It tells you how to react to everyone and everything around you. Your inner voice is powerful. It can destroy a creative goal before it develops into a plan or diminish your confidence to ask for things you deserve.

Your inner voice will not leave you; you cannot break up with it or run away and hope it won't find you. You have to gain awareness of your inner dialogue and train your thoughts to be your biggest source of support and comfort. The conversation you have with self has a larger effect than any words that may come from another. Tell yourself something kind!

Thoughts vs. Emotions
What You Think (Controllable) vs. What You Feel (Uncontrollable)

You can stop a thought midsentence. Try it. Begin using your inner voice to spark a thought about your opinion on school food. Then tell yourself to stop talking. That's control—that's all consciousness. You *can* control your voice and personal narrative.

We are souls that are constantly observing our thoughts. When we master the ability to change or refocus our mind, we begin to gain power over our lives. Have you ever made a poor decision and had a person of authority ask, "What were you thinking?!" as if to imply you weren't thinking at all? They're simply frustrated with your decision to act on impulse without consulting your mind first. More than likely, when you make a poor decision, it's because you're choosing to ignore the healthier ideas of your inner voice.

When you're punished for making a stupid decision, you can't be mad at anyone but yourself! Punishment helps us think about the decisions we've made and how they could have been avoided. Anyone that has a lot of time on their hands has a lot of time to think. Punishment is a tactic to inspire us to use our brains.

There are limits to the decisions you're allowed to make as a teenager. As a young adult, you don't have full control over your life, but you're still the artist, creator, and master of your future and your individual story. Teenagers sometimes think they won't start "living" until they're off to college and on their own, but that's not true. The evolution of your best self begins with the inner work that you're doing now. The thoughts you possess have power over your body, emotions, and daily decisions. Think smart!

Start by paying attention to the times your thoughts are the loudest. *What do you hear?* Sometimes we try our best to ignore the bad thoughts. Explore where your thoughts are coming from. Mindfulness and observation allow you to see your thoughts. Just like a friend who has the blues, sometimes our thoughts just want to be heard. Listen completely and try to understand where they stem from before letting them go. The thoughts we suppress only get louder.

Negative thoughts have the power to produce the following:
1. Aggression
2. Anger
3. Anxiety
4. Desire to use unhealthy forms of comfort
5. Eating disorders
6. Obsessive-compulsive disorder
7. Post-traumatic stress
8. Problems with relationships

When thoughts are harmful or scary, consider speaking them out loud to a therapist or school counselor who can help you analyze them. Finding a trusted therapist is a healthy option for beginning the journey to self-comfort, especially if you have a mental disorder. According to the Mental Heath Association in New York State, signs and symptons of mental health problems begin, on average, at age fourteen.

In order to comfort yourself, you must first understand your needs and where they stem from. Self-reflection can begin by pondering what you'd wish to hear from others. What words or opinions would boost your self-esteem? Start saying those positive phrases to yourself. Someone else's opinion shouldn't be valued more than your own.

Below are some affirmations to help you get started! Write them down in places you frequent. Say them out loud or to yourself until you believe them with all of your heart.

- I want to be better for myself.
- I deserve to be happy.
- I love _____ about myself.
- I'm going to show the world who I am.
- I have great purpose.
- There is no such thing as perfection.

Start each day by looking at yourself in the mirror and saying the words "I see you" out loud. We spend the least amount of time seeing our own physical appearance. We deserve the same attention we give to others when we look them in the eyes as they speak. Tell yourself that you see yourself, because you should see yourself both inside and out as much as possible.

Chapter 3
Remedies and Takeaways:

- #AllThoughtsMatter

- Negate, negate, negate the fears.

- Start with affirmations.

- You cannot suppress your thoughts, but you can control the way you react to them.

- Your mind is handcuffed to the soul. Which opinion do you trust to take the lead?

- Read a book!

- Think, listen, repeat . . . and then question everything.

- You're living your life story. Direct it well!

CHAPTER 4

Bullies and People That Sting

"Body dysmorphia started for me when I was eleven. Every day I'm getting better and better at ignoring my false view of my body, because the truth is, for the longest time, I did not see what other people saw. I was self-shaming."

**—Nazanin Mandi,
model and motivational speaker**

After a lot of years and low moments, Nazanin Mandi eventually came to accept her natural body and committed to working out to stay fit. Her body will never be identical to anyone else's, and loving herself only happened when she began to accept the things she couldn't change and put effort into the things she could (in a healthy way). Today, the former eleven-year-old self-shamer is a beautiful professional model, motivational speaker, and majorly successful swimsuit designer who uses her story of dealing with anxiety and body dysmorphia to uplift and inspire others.

Here are a few questions to ask yourself when you begin to self-shame:

1. How true are the things that you tell yourself? Fact check self-sabotaging thoughts.

_____

_____

_____

2. Why are you giving yourself such a hard time?

_____

_____

_____

3. What/who are you comparing yourself to and why?

_____

_____

_____

You find real friends when you learn how to be your own friend. Tearing yourself down will only cause psychological damage. Don't be an inner bully—do yourself a favor and try a pep talk instead!

Of the million people in
the world who will sign up
to root against you, please
don't volunteer to
be the +1.

Bullying

A bully is an aggressor who feels it's "my way or the highway." They can be violent, verbally abusive, or negative and critical toward others. A bully can be a friend, a classmate, or, in some unfortunate cases, a person living in your home. Bullies threaten others to feel good about themselves or to get what they want, and they typically prey on shy or passive personalities. Most teens have been a victim of bullying, and some admit that they've been guilty of bullying others.

The Bully

Bullying is a big cry for help. Bullies often feel unloved, undesirable, and antisocial. Most bullies are subconsciously fighting to release pain they've been harboring inside. Inflicting pain on others is the most destructive way to self-comfort, yet many people do it because they've experienced others doing it to them.

According to a UCLA psychology study, 30 percent of young people admit to being a bully. If you're a child who bullies, think about why you're doing it and be honest with yourself about your intent. Knowing that you're hurting someone and continuing to do it anyway is unfair to the victim. You're releasing your pain in the worst way, and if you've experienced this type of behavior from someone else, you know firsthand how hurtful it is. Put yourself in the victim's shoes—practicing empathy will help you manage your behavior toward other people.

Empathy: the ability to understand and share the feelings of others

Throughout your life, you'll have to interact with a wide variety of people who carry different thoughts and perspectives. Practicing empathy will help guide those interactions. People often don't pay attention, yet so much can be said through the way we act. For instance, as a bystander, you can learn a lot by trying to understand the emotions and triggers of a bully.

The Victim

Keep your thoughts calm and your circle positive, and never let a bully get inside your head. If you're a victim of mistreatment and bullying, understand that it has nothing to do with you. You can go out of your way to make kind gestures and say hello to someone every single day, but they still might not like you. If people are closed off or uninterested in building a friendship with you, it may simply be that you're not like-minded individuals. Not everyone and everything is for you.

Most bullying takes place in school, on school grounds, or on the school bus. No one is immune to it, not even Taylor Swift. "The kids at school thought it was weird that I liked country [music]," she says. "They'd make fun of me." But no matter how difficult it was, Taylor was honest about her interests, and it was her authentic taste that led her to a career as one of the most successful country singers of all time.

If a fellow student is hassling or making fun of you, you must decide how you'll allow them to make you feel. Unfortunately, you can't control the actions of others. You can, however, tell yourself that some opinions of you are false and unwelcome. Once you decide not to let harmful words affect you, your reaction to them begins to change—and it's usually your reaction that the bully is really looking for.

If you're a victim of any type of bullying, document the behavior of your bully and share it with an appropriate authority figure. Hold people accountable for their actions. In most cases, misbehaving will last as long as the person doesn't get caught.

As a person who was once severely bullied and then became a bully herself, I can tell you that if you allow the tormenting behavior to continue, you're enabling the bully. I remember there was a girl I didn't like in middle school because she was known for "messing around" with a lot of guys and hanging out with other girls' boyfriends. Her actions were none of my business, but I let them upset me and thought that calling her names and belittling her in public would change her behavior. I did this until she told on me and I got in trouble for it. My teachers were disappointed by my ugly behavior, and that made me feel horrible. I wanted to keep a good reputation in school and not to be labeled as a bad person because I knew I wasn't one.

Do Something

Speaking out against bullying is important because bullies often get more aggressive with time. The best solution is to tell a teacher, parent, or school counselor about bullying so they can take action against the inappropriate behavior. It may seem like you're snitching, but you're only protecting the bully and making the situation worse by staying quiet. If you tell an authority figure about the issue and they do nothing, tell somebody else.

Have you ever heard the term "Snitches get stitches"? This term originated with organized criminals who threatened witnesses to keep them silent. A snitch—also known as a tattletale, squealer, informant, or betrayer—is often seen in a bad light for speaking out against something that is wrong. However, sometimes *not* speaking up causes a bigger threat to you and others. Remember chapter 3—think smart! Don't let fear rule your decisions. If you're a victim of bullying, understand that the real problem lies inside the person doing the harm. Put your safety first and follow your intuition.

Trust in a school counselor as a resource for these situations. They are trained to deal with these difficult interactions, and it's something they must act on as part of their job. The counselor can provide advice for dealing with unwanted harassment. It's also great to privately advise your teacher of what's going on if bullying behavior is happening within the classroom. Being distracted from schoolwork because of bullying isn't something your teacher should ever allow.

You have a right to be happy and feel safe at school and at home. Unfortunately, if you stand up for yourself by reacting in the same manner as the bully, you could end up putting yourself in greater harm. It's not worth it unless you truly have your back up against the wall and no other option but to protect yourself. Otherwise, walk away. Consult an authority figure. Be the bigger person. Know that the words of others won't stay with you in your adulthood. Many of the most successful people in this world were once bullied.

Hurting others
provides temporary
satisfaction to people with
troubled minds. Once you
understand this, you'll spend
less time reacting
to people who
hurt you.

Cyberbullying

One of today's most popular forms of harassment is cyberbullying. Cyberbullying involves harassing or bullying someone online. Think of all the people who excitedly write negative comments on celebrity-gossip pages for no good reason. They're basking in the perceived failure or flaws of others because it makes them feel better about themselves. How crazy is it that we live in a world where you can hurt the feelings of complete strangers?

The internet makes it easy to hide behind bad behavior. Not only do children misuse social media, but we also live in a time where adult predators create fake identities to lure in minors, retrieve their personal information and photos, and even cause them harm. You have to be careful how you engage online and with whom.

Cyberbullying comes in many forms. Some bullies take a screenshot of someone, share it with others, and privately belittle or criticize them. Be careful what you say and send via text or private message, and know that things you delete do not always disappear. Any form of bullying on the internet is documentable behavior that can come back to haunt the bully.

Circulating unflattering, violent, or sexually suggestive photos of others is another form of bullying. You may think sharing such a photo is all in fun, but consider whether or not the person in the photo would approve of you spreading it around. Without permission to share private photos or information, you're putting both the other person and yourself at risk. Cyberbullying can cause people to self-harm, experience low self-esteem and anxiety, or worse.

Thankfully, many states have passed laws to protect the rights of victims of cyberbullying. One time, in the midst of a Level 10 Breakup (see chapter 10 for more on breakups), my guy created a fake number in an attempt to catfish me (trick me into thinking he was someone else) and retrieve photos and information that he could share with other guys. It was all a revenge plot, spurred by his broken heart and seriously messed-up motives. As soon as I became aware of the attempt to catfish me, I filed a police report so they'd have a record of the harassment. Under certain circumstances, bullies and their parents can face legal charges. If the bullying was sexual in nature or involved sexting, the person responsible could be registered as a sex offender. That's something that will never leave their record.

Remember: Bullies can use any number of tactics to harass others online, from posts on message boards to direct messaging to fake web pages to photo sharing. If you believe you've been a victim of this type of behavior, I urge you to report it.

Gossip

Gossip is another form of bullying. You can't avoid being a victim of gossip, but you *can* give people less to talk about. Try not to say or do anything that you wouldn't want the entire school to find out about. Be careful with the personal things you share and the personal things you *do* with other people. Sometimes people gossip when things they see or hear make them uncomfortable. Most times, people gossip simply because they have insecurities and jealousies—talking about someone else makes them feel good about themselves. Don't give them fuel for their gossip bonfire.

"I don't really care what people think of me. I know the girls don't like me for whatever reason, but that's because they're probably unhappy with themselves."

—Sydney M., sixteen years old

No words, opinions, or hate can define you. The only way the words of others can hurt and affect you is if you begin to consider those words to be true or react to them. When you know something isn't true, just let it be. Sometimes, no matter how many times you try to correct the story or fix the facts, others simply won't hear you out. If the gossip is true and it's something you can't take back, being hard on yourself will only make it worse. Learn from the lesson, forgive yourself, and move on.

Then, learn to stay away from people who talk about people and not things. There is no gain in joining the gossip gang. Find a better affiliation.

Make a concerted effort to stop gossip before it leaves your lips. Set a good example for your peer group. If you're hanging out with others and the conversation turns to gossip, either excuse yourself or, better yet, say something positive about the person who's being targeted. Another tactic is to ask the person why they're speaking badly about the other. That forces the gossiper to look at themselves. Rising above gossip is one of the most mature choices you can make as a young adult.

#ByeBully

Bullies want to get a reaction out of people. They're trying to transfer their pain. Protect your peace and speak up for yourself and others. Find the confidence to be assertive without being aggressive. It's one of the greatest forms of bully repellent.

Where is your bully-free zone? Everyone has a peaceful place that's safe from bullies. This might be your room, a local community center, a church, a library, a club at school, or a family member's house. Wherever you feel most safe is where you should spend more time.

Where are your bully-free zones?

_____

_____

_____

Easy steps to anti-bully behavior:

- Pay attention to people and try to include everyone present in the conversation.
- Befriend the new kid in school.
- If you don't have anything nice to say . . .
- Go out of your way to say hello and acknowledge the shy kids.
- When people are gossiping about someone, excuse yourself from the conversation or say something nice about the person.
- If you think you've bullied someone in the past, make amends. It's never too late for an apology. It might not be important to you, but victims of bullying never forget their experiences.
- If you see something, say something.

Chapter 4
Remedies and Takeaways:

- Don't bully yourself!

- Empathetic people always experience advancement.

- Bullies are hurt people with troubled minds.

- Do not make excuses or feel bad for bullies. Hold them accountable for their behavior, or it won't end.

- Be careful with the personal things you share and do with others. Secrets aren't always safe forever.

- What happens on the internet does not always stay on the internet.

- You have a right to live bully-free.

- Being assertive without being aggressive = bully repellent.

CHAPTER 5

What's Normal, Anyway?

"We don't have to fit ourselves into someone else's idea of how we should be. You are your own person, and you're the only you that has ever been or will ever be."

—Miguel, Grammy-winning musician
and PDF guest speaker

The *Oxford English Dictionary* defines "normal" as conforming to a standard or the common type; usual, typical, or expected.

But who sets the standard? Who decides what's socially acceptable, and how did they get appointed to make these decisions?!

I aspired to be normal (or common) for most of my childhood. I had full, curly hair that I was afraid to wear down because no one in my school had hair like me, I hated smiling in pictures because of my gummy grin, *and* I was part of the itty-bitty titty committee (none of these things ever changed). My head was two times the average size, and I was so skinny I'd wear multiple pairs of leggings underneath my jeans so that I would look like the rest of the girls. I was different, and I still am.

It is exhausting trying to please other people. I woke up one day and realized I couldn't stand out by trying to blend in. Instead, I found self-esteem in loving myself and the things that made me unique, regardless of anyone else's opinion. I eventually started to laugh at the jokes people made about me because some were actually funny. Confidence didn't come overnight, but I wanted to like myself. I wanted to feel good, or at least pretend I did.

Once I accepted the things I couldn't change about myself, I gained self-esteem. Once I allowed others to see the real me and didn't bother to explain myself, I had a true transformation.

How do you find acceptance for the things you cannot change? Recognize reality. You have the ability to modify some things about yourself or improve your behavior, but who you are at the core will never change. Your DNA is not a mistake, and you'll enjoy life more when you begin surrounding yourself with people who appreciate you for you.

It will also help your self-confidence to connect with others who share your interests and perspectives. Those with similar points of view can help build you up and affirm you. I'm not saying you should avoid everyone who has a different opinion or outlook, but it helps to find friends that you share a good deal of common ground with. In college and in the workplace, you'll have to engage with people from all walks of life—but as a teen, you're still trying to find yourself, and it's helpful to feel comfortable among your peers.

"Trying to please everyone is
a stressful life."

—Andre 3000

Your Look

Normality is a personal point of view.

Have you ever thought to yourself, *I'm too tall, I'm too skinny, I'm too fat, I hate this unibrow*? You will go through many physically awkward stages as a young adult. It's hard to love your body as it's changing so vastly (especially when you hit puberty).

When you start comparing yourself to peers or images in the media, it's normal to think that your brain and body aren't good enough, even though you're often comparing yourself to false realities or filtered images. What is real and true? If you are unsure, how can you compare your own truth to what you see?

It is common to feel uncomfortable in your own skin. In fact, many adults are still not content with their physical appearance. Women spend billions of dollars on beauty products each year, and some will go to extremes and get cosmetic procedures. We often envy the features of others, yet even those we view as "flawless" probably have their own insecurities.

Self-esteem centered around your appearance will almost always leave you feeling unsatisfied.

You cannot build your self-esteem while focusing on what you don't like.

Before you answer the questions below, ask yourself if you're ready to transform your thoughts into positive ones. If you are not committed, the doubt will control any progress you wish to make.

It makes me feel good when people tell me I am . . .

_____

_____

_____

I am learning to accept my...

_____

_____

_____

_____

Acceptance matters when it's a personal opinion of yourself.

PRACTICE
NONCONFORMITY

Find your brave. The discovery of self is the beginning of liberation. In learning who you are, you'll uncover where you belong and where you're most accepted. There's peace to be found there, and it makes dealing with all the other stresses of the world so much easier.

Even the way you think should feel different. You probably define yourself through your tastes, desires, and hobbies. These are the things that help you stand out from the crowd. Many famous musicians, artists, scientists, and influencers have achieved success *because* they were different. People with groundbreaking ideas are the ones who walked their own path, sometimes resulting in their helping countless people or making millions.

It's healthy to embrace your quirks, and the easiest way to do that is by finding others who share those quirks and calling them friends. But if it seems like you're an anomaly in your environment, then just do you without fear of judgment!

If you have trouble finding people in your community who relate to your thoughts—do you!

If you don't want to play sports and would rather collect rocks because your ultimate goal in life is to be a geologist—that's awesome!

If you don't dress like the rest of the kids because your personal style is creative—do you!

If you learn differently from others and people make fun of you because they have no life, who cares!?—Do you!

And if you view someone as perfect, it's just because they hide their flaws well. Please, continue to do you!

People will only reveal what they want you to know.

Take social media, for example.

Do you know someone who posts about their losses or glorifies the things they wish they could change? I don't. Filters and photo-editing apps were invented so people could pose as their own version of perfect. People can create an alternate reality, personality, or physical appearance; but just as video games are not real, neither is everything that's shared on your social feed. Everyone is hiding their flaws and rejecting acceptance one post at a time. Since this world is being lived in both reality and online, you must be suspicious of it all.

You don't live in social media, you live here. Social media should come with a warning. People instinctively want a pat on the back for looking nice or accomplishing something, but feeling good about yourself should be enough. Through social media, you can become dependent on receiving the approval of others. Needing someone else to make you feel good reverses the work you're doing to build yourself up. In order to self-comfort, you need to believe your opinion of yourself is enough.

You can be one of many or one of one.

Stop comparing your life and personal attributes to others'. Everyone wants what they don't have. Commit to the idea that everything you need you already possess inside, and know that your self-worth will play a major part in how you advance in personal and professional relationships.

Chapter 5
Remedies and Takeaways:

- "Normal" is defined as conforming to a standard; usual, typical, or expected.

- Hiding your truth from others makes it harder to learn to love yourself.

- Find your brave.

- Comparison is destructive.

- Embrace your quirks and unique characteristics.

- Be careful not to become reliant on validation from others through social media.

- Acceptance begins with you. Wherever it's not found is not worth your time.

- Like yourself first.

CHAPTER 6

How We're Raised

"My stepmom was a gambler who made horrible financial decisions. She would even take my money, and one day when I wouldn't give her my allowance she beat me until my nose bled. That was the day I finally told my dad about the abuse, and after that it never happened again. I should've told him sooner."
—Jatali Brit, author and founder of Kids Who Bank

The first examples of how to (and how not to) love come from our family. We hold our parents or guardians to the highest standard and expect them to be our biggest source of love. But what if our parents fail to meet our expectations and leave us disappointed?

Parents make mistakes, even though most have great intentions. Most parents aspire to help their children become better individuals, but some just don't know how. **Our parents and guardians may be struggling with their own identities or happiness, which prevents them from putting us first. Furthermore, their ability to be positive role models may depend on what they experienced in their childhoods and where they**

are in their own lives.

How much do you know about your parents? Is their parenting style similar to what they experienced as a child? As little children, we constantly ask our parents *why* about everything. As we get older, the questions often peter out, and we never get around to asking our parents much about themselves and their relationship with us. It's okay to ask questions in order to understand your parents' motives and *why* they have chosen their parenting style. If you want to strengthen the relationship, the best thing you can do is try. No matter what happens as a result of asking, you'll at least know you made an effort.

Name your parents/guardians.

_____

_____

What do you know about how they were raised and who they were as children?

_____

_____

_____

_____

Ask your parents or guardians to tell you what they're most passionate about and list the things that make them happy (that don't include you).

_____

_____

_____

How are you and your parents/guardians similar or different?

_____

_____

_____

I once interviewed a twelve-year-old boy named Dylan who was raised in a wealthy household, sat courtside at NBA games, and spent his summers in the French Riviera. Although many children would envy his lifestyle, Dylan wouldn't say he'd had it easy. He was the product of a workaholic father who wouldn't put the phone down for more than five minutes to give him the attention he yearned for. So Dylan acted out in school and rebelled against authority.

Stop and think about his dad's point of view. The obsessive work habits were likely based on his desire to provide a certain lifestyle for his family. Where the parent finds it important to work, the child may feel abandoned and neglected.

When intent is misinterpreted in the household, communication has to happen.

If you're yearning for more time and attention, you have to express that to your absent parent or guardian. You cannot blame them for behavior that bothers you if they're unaware of how you feel. Sometimes parents may brush off our complaints, so try expressing your emotions in a mature manner. For instance: "When you're not present I don't feel loved, and it affects me in the way I . . ." This strategy of calm communication can also help in situations when you feel your parent is overbearing or unsupportive. Before you start the conversation, make sure you're prepared to offer a couple solutions to your parent that you feel are fair for both parties.

Communicating your feelings is the first step toward rectifying the situation. Regardless of how your parent responds to your request, your voice is at least being heard. You deserve to share with people how they make you feel as long as it's done respectfully.

A Parent's Discipline

It's difficult for many parents to master the balance between discipline and reward. People don't need a license to become parents, and while you're learning to understand your unique self, your parents are also learning you. Sometimes you may feel their need to protect you restricts your ability to express yourself and your freedom to grow. As much as you may disagree with their decisions, when your elders have good intentions, you have to respect them.

Many times, the adults with the strictest rules and expectations for us are our biggest allies. Unfortunately, some teens won't understand that until they're mature enough to realize that their guardians only wanted to help them be better. It's a great thing to have someone who wants what's best for you. Don't take that for granted.

Everyone has experienced some type of punishment. Has your parent or guardian ever said that one day you'll understand or be grateful for their disciplinary actions? In most cases, they're right. If you fail a test and get punished, your parents are only conditioning you to work harder and be more prepared for the real world. As an adult, if you fail at your task in the workplace, you may not receive multiple chances to do better. You must work smart, come prepared, and do your best to continuously impress your supervisors. If you don't, well, you'll get fired. The real world doesn't owe you any second chances to make careless mistakes.

Next time you get upset with your parents, remember that they have one of the toughest jobs in the world and that they truly do love you.

No matter how absent or present a parent is in your life, it's impossible for them not to love you—you're a part of them and their greatest contribution to the world. You don't need to hear what you already feel. Know it in your heart. Take pride in knowing that even if your parents mess up, they did one amazing thing—they had you. Grow up and do beautiful things with your gifts and talents, whether your parents acknowledge them or not.

I am the result
of my parents doing
a good deed for the world.

#ParentsArePeople

Your parents may say things they don't mean. They may suffer from an inability to use healthy coping mechanisms for stress. They may not have had a great example of parenting to refer to. Recognize that they're people navigating through life. They just happen to be who you call Mom or Dad.

Chapter 6
Remedies and Takeaways:

- Lofty expectations can lead to disappointment.

- Your parents love you, even if they don't say or show it.

- Guardians are people who don't receive enough credit for their love and commitment.

- As you learn yourself, remember to take time to learn your parents so you can see how you're similar and different.

- You can't understand someone until you've been in their shoes. The job of a parent is the hardest job in the world.

CHAPTER 7

Don't Hurt Yourself

"When I was fifteen, I woke up in Bellevue Hospital because I tried to harm myself."

—Yaya M., producer and event curator

When I was a teenager, I had a friend who cut herself. She used sharp objects to break the skin on her wrist and let it bleed. We were in tenth grade. I didn't quite understand that there was an intent behind cutting oneself other than causing discomfort. I knew that cutting could potentially lead to death. It was hard to understand how someone who seemed to have it all was battling with depression and acting like they were worthless. It was even harder to accept because she was my best friend and I didn't see any warning signs.

The first time I noticed the Band-Aids, I asked what was going on. I remember my friend explaining that she felt depressed because of her parents' divorce and was overwhelmed by the demand to excel in school. It was evident that her cutting was a cry for attention. She covered up the cuts with really cool Band-Aids covered in cartoon characters and acted as if they were a fashion statement, but she ultimately was only calling more attention to her self-inflicted injuries.

One of the activities for Precious Dreams Foundation youth is pillow-case decorating. The objective is to think of everything that fuels positive thinking and to illustrate or write these things on the pillow. This activity helps inspire happy thoughts and dreams for our youth, who often live in places that cause stress. On a visit to the Children's Center, I met a sixteen-year-old foster child who wrote a poem on her pillowcase about cutting. I knew right away that she was a cutter because I could see scars all over her arms. "I'm not good enough to be loved. Not good enough to be cared for . . ."

It was a sad poem, but the teen girl said writing out the words reminded her of her mental state during the time of her deepest depression and the pillowcase activity showed her how far she'd come. Even though she was overcoming her painful past, she shared with our volunteers that she got teased because of her scars, which made coping with her illness harder. The memory of her decision to cut was one she'd never be able to escape.

Cutting is part of a category of behaviors called non-suicidal self-injury. I'm addressing this because one in five people has attempted to cut themselves at some point in their lives. NSSI also includes skin-picking, scratching, biting, and burning. Cutters often feel that causing pain on the outside calms their emotional distress or anxiety. A small percentage do it as avoidance (a distraction from their current issues), and some even cut in order to punish themselves.

When a person uses something harmful to comfort themselves, they're creating a much bigger problem.

Cutting can lead to further psychological damage, as well as potentially embarrassing physical scars. It is a very dangerous coping mechanism. To resist self-abuse, you have to prioritize finding solutions and healthy coping mechanisms. Everything is going to be okay as long as you want it to be. If you're self-harming, make a list of things to try next time you have the self-inflicting thoughts. The alternatives won't always work but you may find success with one of the options when you need it most.

Here are some suggestions:

- Try scribbling over a piece of paper and fill the entire paper with the ink from top to bottom.
- If you're cutting to numb your pain, try holding a piece of ice until you can't feel your hand anymore. This isn't fun, but it's better than putting your life at risk.
- Run. Don't run away from your problems, but get moving, go outside, and run away from the space that inspired the bad thoughts. Run fast and far, until you can't run anymore.
- Tell a friend or trusted family member what you're doing and ask if you can call and vent to them next time you're feeling low. It's hard to deal with any bottled-up emotion. The first step of simply telling someone what's going on will cause a bit of temporary relief. If you're afraid they will judge you, start your confession with, "Please don't judge me, but I need to share something with you and I need your help."

If you find difficulty in finding an option that works for you, then the next step is talking to a mental-health specialist.

Other people may be the reason we seek to harm ourselves. Disappointments or prior abuse can result in depressive and negative emotions. Whatever the case, you have the power to choose to fall victim to your problems *or* turn your story into one of the greatest outcomes of all time. Attempting suicide robs you of experiencing your happy ending.

Grow through it.
Go through it.
Keep going.

Dealing with Depression

Self-harming thoughts often stem from depression. "Depression" is a word people often use to diagnose themselves when they're feeling down about something that they can't control. However, it's a serious disorder that looks different for everyone.

What are signs of depression?

- Lack of motivation to do daily activities
- Loss of energy
- Self-loathing
- Continuous feelings of sadness, hopelessness, agitation, or anger
- Change in eating or sleeping habits
- Withdrawal from friends and family
- An inclination to be alone rather than interact with others
- Suicidal thoughts

Symptoms must be present for at least two weeks in order for you to be diagnosed with depression, but keep in mind it can come in waves and is not necessarily consistent.

Depression does not mean that you're a failure. In fact, if you think you're suffering from depression, it may be caused by something that's completely out of your control such as hormones, inherited traits, biological chemistry, or past experiences of trauma. Recent surveys indicate about 20 percent of all teens experience depression before they reach adulthood.

Depression is draining not only for you but also for the people closest to you. Recognizing the need for help is the first step to recovery for all things. Don't count on others to identify your depression and act on your behalf—since depression is different for everyone, your loved ones may not even know you are suffering. Take action to help yourself by speaking out and seeking assistance. Start by seeing a psychiatrist or psychologist who can diagnose you with a specific form of depression. They will advise you on the best treatment. Then, commit to following through with the treatment, and have patience with yourself because it's going to take a lot of work.

Self-Comfort through Depression

- Eliminate harmful or toxic relationships or avoid people that trigger stressful thoughts. If you're forced to be around these types of people in school or at home, try to find every available opportunity to be away from them when possible.
- Don't push away the good people. You'll regret it later. If someone is prying into your life because they care, don't treat them like a nuisance. Express your need for privacy until you're ready to share.
- Dive into the things you love. Fill your calendar with activities and events that give you peace.
- Write down how you're feeling if you're not comfortable sharing it with anyone else. Keep your writing in a safe place. Any type of expression is better than suppression.
- Do daily good deeds. Helping people helps.

Feeling Mad

Have you ever been so angry you punched a wall? I bet that hurt. There are times in our lives when we react poorly to things, even if we are not experiencing depression. Fears and anxiety can drive us mad. It happens all the time, and there's nothing wrong with making mistakes as long as we learn from them. The ability to look back on a bad decision and see your growth since that moment is a feeling we can all appreciate. Don't be hard on yourself for learning a lesson the hard way.

Live—because life has so much to offer. Live for all the people who have hurt you and didn't want you to win in life. Live to prove them wrong. Keep going because your past doesn't define you. Live knowing that every single day is a chance to start over.

Once you decide the type of life you want to live, start talking (to yourself).

(Come on—I dare you to write the most positive and egotistical, Kanye-inspired thoughts about yourself here.)

DEAR SELF,

I am . . .

I am the best at . . .

I know that no one else can compare to me because . . .

Cut and paste images/words here that are a representation of your best self, your future self, and your goals.

Did that feel good, recognizing your strengths?

Forget the noise around you. This is your world, and the thoughts that matter are the ones inside of you. You must decide now that you want to live, survive, and thrive in this life. If negative or harmful thoughts are holding you back despite your efforts to overcome them, consider seeking medical assistance. We're not supposed to overcome all of our problems alone. Being able to self-comfort does _not_ mean you can cure disease or mental illness.

That said, even if you do decide to enlist the help of other people, you can still do a lot of the legwork on your own.

#HelpYourself

So often we hold ourselves to an all-or-nothing standard. Don't reduce yourself to nothing just because you can't get something. If you indulge in negative self-talk, the results always leave you feeling worthless. Do not punish yourself for mistakes. When you fall, other people can help you get up, but no one can help you plant your feet firmly on the ground. You are the only person who holds that power . . . so why wait for a hand to give you a boost?

Take small steps to get out of a negative headspace.

1. Reach out to a good listener. We don't always want or need advice. Just find someone who cares about you and will provide an ear without making you feel judged.
2. Avoid foods that can adversely affect your moods, like trans fats,

sugar, and refined carbs.

3. Go outside.
4. Get rid of objects that can harm you. Do it yourself or ask others to do it for you.
5. Love on a pet. Find comfort in an animal.

Ugly situations will pass. If you're criticizing yourself because of things you've done in the past, let them go. Forgive yourself instead of harming yourself, and start anew. Don't let limiting beliefs manifest. "I can't do anything right," "I'll never be good enough," "Nobody likes me"—these are all lies you tell yourself to cope, and they reverse all steps taken toward self-comfort.

You are good enough. You are strong. Find your faith, and never let anyone take it away from you. People who don't value your life must be kept at a far distance at all times. Believe in your life and promote life for others. We all deserve to live.

The National Suicide Prevention Lifeline is available 24 hours every day at (800) 273-8255. It provides free and confidential support for people in distress as well as prevention and crisis resources for you and your loved ones. <3

If you believe someone you know may be suicidal, speak up and tell an adult immediately. Saving a life is always better than keeping a secret.

Chapter 7
Remedies and Takeaways:

- Self-harm is self-hate. You deserve better.

- What's normal? Depression: 20 percent of all teens experience depression before they reach adulthood.

- Practice self-forgiveness.

- Dive into the things that you love and surround yourself with people who lift you up.

- Don't let anyone convince you to keep a secret that harms someone.

- As hard as life may seem, if you're alive, you have an opportunity to turn it around.

- If you know someone in need of help, do something!

CHAPTER 8

Higher Calling, Higher Education

"The most delicious flavor in life is, 'I told you so.'"
—Gary Vaynerchuk, serial entrepreneur
and CEO of VaynerMedia

To reach your "I told you so" moment, you have to do the work and climb the ladder. Your ladder right now is your education. That resource for brain food is where you can discover your gifts, higher calling, and basic tools to get by in life.

School—the place for escape or the place we feel forced to go. Just like life, our opinion of school depends on our experiences (both inside and outside the classroom). School is an opportunity to experiment and learn a wide range of subjects. It's the foundation on which all grand achievements are made. It is also a place that allows you the freedom to showcase your strengths, work on your weaknesses, and thrive.

In life, no one is going to take a red marker, cross out all of your mistakes, show you how to correct them and help you succeed for free. Education is key for lifelong wellness and a future full of prosperity. Education is the process of facilitating learning—the acquisition of knowledge, skills, values, beliefs, and habits.

In school, you'll often take classes that seem tedious, but don't lose your curiosity in everything. Take advantage of the *now* and the opportunity to educate yourself on various subjects. This is the time to learn what you like while the consequences of failure are relatively small. It's bigger than getting into a dream college or university—getting an education and building your work ethic prepares you to succeed in a career and as a responsible human being. Your grades are a result of your commitment to your work. Some subjects may not come easily and will require discipline and extra studying time to understand.

We often find motivation in accomplishment. Perhaps you tend to lose your motivation when you aren't meeting *or exceeding* your own expectations. Nobody wants to lose, but not doing well at something should motivate you to try harder, not give up. Life is set up in a way where we lose at many things repeatedly, but it's all part of learning how to win.

#LearnToLose

Getting an education is your first investment in yourself. Investing in yourself will attract other people to support your dreams. When a teacher, boss, potential investor, or sponsor sees your willingness to better yourself, they will commit to helping you achieve greatness, but no one will cosign someone who's all talk and no results. You have to show proof.

Extracurricular activities and after-school programs have saved many lives.

For some teens, extracurricular activities provide motivation to attend and do well in school. When positive outlets are provided, healthy habits are formed. Involving yourself in social groups, clubs, and sports comes with major mental and physical benefits. It's a great way to discover your individual personality and skills. Many children use these options as an outlet for stress or a way to avoid trouble, drug abuse, loneliness, and unwanted feelings. Get active!

One of the best ways to self-comfort is by participating in an activity that produces positive results or focuses your thoughts on something that helps you develop a skill or talent. Take advantage of everything your school has to offer, but be careful not to overschedule. Cramming too many things into your calendar can cause stress and create expectations that you can't physically and mentally reach. Get busy, but be realistic and don't spread yourself too thin.

Discovering purpose through extracurricular activities is a major self-esteem booster and also prepares you for your future. Top colleges are usually impressed with students who have committed themselves to developing hobbies and skills outside the classroom. Students involved in activities by choice are well-rounded and responsible.

What school teams, afterschool activities, or clubs are you currently involved in?

_____

_____

_____

What can you participate in that will help you explore a new passion or meet new people? You don't have to be good at something to TRY(out).

_____

_____

_____

Let's talk about why you wouldn't like school.

Do alarm clocks irk your soul? My alarm clock was a trigger for negative thoughts. I'm still not someone who likes to be woken up before I'm ready. In fact, if you need an alarm to wake up, they say that means you aren't getting enough rest (refer to chapter 19 for more sleep talk). Not everyone is a morning person, but everyone has to learn how to function in the morning. Important things happen there.

Adults usually need coffee for an energy boost before going to work, yet students are expected to find their morning optimism on their own. Jump up, get dressed, perform! Teens are expected to just have it all together (especially in the morning). Young people may have more energy than adults, but that doesn't make a difference if they aren't getting a proper night's rest.

Aside from sleep-related challenges, you may have other reasons for disliking school. If that's the case, it's possible you fall under one or more of these categories:

1. You have a learning disability.
2. You're trying your hardest but the work seems too difficult.
3. You're more interested in a passion or talent that isn't being used in each class.
4. You'd rather stay home and be lazy.
5. You're experiencing social issues with peers or a teacher.

Let's go through these issues one at a time.

1. You have some type of learning disability.
Learning disabilities can interfere with a child's ability to focus or influence the way they learn, but they have nothing to do with intelligence. If you think you may have a disability, get tested. Everyone learns at a different pace, and we all have different preferences in teaching styles. But since we can't select our teachers, we have to adjust to the style that's being offered. You'll get lost and left behind if you aren't honest with your teachers about your struggles to keep up with your peers. Figuring out the best way to process information has to be important to you in order for you to be honest about your shortcomings.

According to the National Center for Learning Disabilities (NCLD), one in five children has learning and attention issues or brain-based challenges in reading, writing, math, organization, focus, listening comprehension, social skills, motor skills, or a combination of these. Learning disabilities fall on a spectrum from mild to severe. I personally have a mild case of ADHD and faced many challenges in school because I had a difficult time retaining information unless I wrote it down.

2. and 3. You're trying your hardest but the work seems too difficult, or you're more interested in a passion or talent that isn't being used in each class.

There's a ton of pressure to perform well in school, no matter if a subject comes naturally to you or if it's difficult to digest. Everyone has areas of strength and weakness. Creative people may struggle in math and history but excel in areas where they can showcase their talents. However, every creative person needs a business mindset in order to succeed, so those dreaded math courses really *are* necessary. If you're struggling with a certain subject, you may need a tutor, individualized attention, or a disciplined study schedule to go over what you learn each day. Tell your parents or teachers that you need additional resources to help with homework and keep up with the lessons. Don't ever waste time falling behind. You are not the only person that suffers from this. It's always better to ask for help.

School might not even teach you what you really want to know. It won't always instruct you on how to make money or be an entrepreneur, but having an education will teach you many useful ways to manage your career. Don't risk being taken advantage of or overlooked because of lack of knowledge.

WHAT IS YOUR LEARNING PREFERENCE?

VISUAL

VERBAL

AURAL

PHYSICAL

LOGICAL

SOCIAL

SOLITARY

4. You'd rather stay home and be lazy.

Ask yourself where this will take you in life. How will you find success and make a living based on laziness? Sometimes we find satisfaction in short-term solutions that can have long-term negative effects. Always push through and think about how your decisions will impact your future. School gives you the tools to design a happy reality. Consequences and repercussions of laziness will ruin those plans. No one can help you if you don't want to help yourself. A minimal education is required even if your job is writing captions for social sites.

5. You're experiencing social issues with peers or a teacher.

We all have favorite teachers and teachers we struggle with. Being able to adjust to different surroundings and learning techniques prepares you for life. In the workplace, there will be coworkers or people we report to who we may not have chosen for our summer camp dodgeball team (let alone a major work project!), but we're stuck with them anyway. If switching classes or schools is not an option, you have to focus on the positive and not waste time being unproductive.

It's also very normal to have social issues with peers. Such issues can make it difficult to concentrate or cause feelings of annoyance or frustration. You have to get these people out of your head by learning to block their energy. Don't give them the power of occupying the mind space you need to focus in school. Will they be relevant in 5 years? If not, treat them as such.

Life is many things, but it's never consistent. As you have good days, you'll also have bad. Learn to laugh at the bad stuff, and appreciate every second of the good—because the days will continue to change and life will go on, but your current circumstances won't last forever.

Keep Going

The world is full of distractions and quick ways to make money. However, be careful not to sell yourself a dream of temporary success or stability. Social media is a great example of how someone can secure a large following with no guarantee of future success, health benefits, or a 401k. Many people rely on their popularity, relationships, and followers to provide them with a successful platform, but without a thorough business plan and education, they'll struggle when things hit the fan. Think beyond popularity. If you don't own YouTube, don't rely on your YouTube page being accessible forever. Create your own platform of success and do your research to continuously stay ahead of the trends.

Now is the time to gain as much knowledge as possible. Long-term success will only find those who are prepared and doing the work when nobody is watching. Preparation is a result of education and discipline, and discipline comes from self-talk. You spend approximately thirty-five hours a week in school, not including time spent on homework. Enjoy school for what it's worth, and build a happy life around it.

Chapter 8
Remedies and Takeaways:

- Want to discover what your options are for the future? Go to school.

- Investing in yourself will attract other people to support your dreams.

- Your grades are a result of your commitment to your work.

- Don't be embarrassed to ask for help. A good teacher prefers you to ask questions.

- Everyone learns at a different pace.

- Adults will tell you that you need an education for everything that you want to do In life, and they're telling the truth.

- Your mind is your key to success.

CHAPTER 9

Building Character

"I was raised around someone who broke me down to where I thought nothing of myself. People would tell me I was pretty, and I'd always find a way to not accept the compliment because when I looked in the mirror I saw something different."

—Martine Harris, Gr8 Eight cofounder and speech and language pathologist

Character: the way someone thinks, feels, and behaves.

I titled this chapter "Building Character" because who you are is totally up to you! You're not a victim of anyone else's opinion. You're whoever you decide to be right now, in this moment. Who you are will change as you mature, and it will not always make others feel comfortable. You are not your parents, siblings, or friends. You were created to have an impact on this world once you learn your capabilities and character.

When you look
in the mirror,
do you see yourself
or the opinions
of others?

I did an experiment during an event where I asked children to raise their hands if they knew someone who was gay. About 90 percent of the children in the room raised their hands, and then about half of the students without their hands up started laughing. I asked the kids to explain why they were laughing, and the only explanation they could give was that "it's just funny." Should gay people think they're funny because people who are unfamiliar with them laugh at their expense? No. We all know that being gay doesn't make you a punchline. Gay doesn't mean you're deserving of ridicule or laughter. Immediately, I understood why so many people were afraid to come out about their sexual preference.

It's hard to identify who you are when you're being judged by others for being authentic or confident about your beliefs. Sometimes your friends or family will criticize you more than others, and their criticism might sting the most. You have to get to a point of understanding that the liberation felt in expressing truth feels better than masking your individuality. There are people out there who are like you in certain ways and will be accepting of your differences.

For many people who grow up in a small town or are the victim of a reputation they didn't ask for, going off to college will feel like a second chance at life. I grew up in a town with a population of 9,000 where it was normal for everyone to talk and dress the same. I hated it. I moved across the country for college and began finding and making friends with people who were just like me. I was relieved to know that I could feel comfortable and inspired around like-minded individuals. I didn't have to convince anyone to accept me or dumb anything down to make others feel secure.

If you learn who you are, you will learn where you're going!

Being free to express yourself is what brings you closer to self-love and acceptance. In building your self-esteem, you'll create a safe space to build character and reveal what makes you unique and gives you purpose. Then, once you figure out what makes you feel good, protect it at all costs. This is where you'll find the most joy in life: in spaces that allow you to feel liberated and important.

#ThisIsMe
(LOVE it or LEAVE it)

Where do you feel the most comfortable expressing yourself?

_____

_____

_____

What is something you hide or downplay about yourself to make others feel comfortable?

_____

_____

_____

What are some spaces online or places in your community where people share your interests? Follow the people who motivate you to be your best self.

_____

_____

_____

Would you believe me if I said your character is more important than your skills? You are the sum of the choices you make, and there's much pride to be found in knowing you're a good person. As you learn yourself, start paying attention to your motives and only speak necessary truths. There are no benefits to hiding, lying, and being silent about things your mind wishes to shout. Live your truth, but at the same time, recognize that you're not perfect and will have days when you falter from your true self and make mistakes. Acknowledge those mistakes, but realize that they don't define you.

When I was 15, I shoplifted something that I could afford because I was trying to fit in with a group of girls that almost got me arrested. I actually thought to myself, "Why pay for something if I can get it for free?" and then realized I'd rather be free than in jail any day! I learned my lesson and never repeated it. However, although I did something bad one time, I wouldn't say it's a representation of who I am. I learned fast, forgave myself, and moved on. It's never too late to have a shift in character. I could've been labeled as a shoplifter but instead I'm a philanthropist—go figure!

Staying true to yourself and building character isn't always easy. Do you feel better about results you worked hard for or things you gave little effort and didn't try your best at? If you know someone is in a dangerous situation, would you seek to get them help or pretend not to know what was happening? These are the types of decisions you'll be forced to make that help you build character.

After you begin to discover yourself, start to consider how you present yourself to the world. How does your energy affect others? Do you provide a safe space for others to reveal their true character? Are you easily pulled "out of character"?

As you practice self-talk, you should start with reminding yourself of who you want to be at your greatest potential. Don't let anyone influence you to be less. Perhaps you'll notice that the times you act "out of character" are the times you're peer pressured or triggered by something.

A trigger causes a negative emotional response and reignites memories of trauma. Triggers are very personal and unique to each individual. Personally, when I hear people yell, it makes me run away and shut down.

Trigger Reason and Reaction: My father's side of the family used to argue and fight all the time. Even in basic conversation, they yelled over each other. I hated it. As a result, I don't listen when people yell and don't care to explain to them why it's a problem. Instead, I leave. Yelling triggers within me the instant desire to escape.

Take notice and communicate what bothers you. Is the trigger leading to something harmful and real, or is it a false alarm going off in your head because of something you've experienced in the past? Your past helps you protect yourself from future danger, but be sure you're not using that protective instinct to treat others like they were participants in your past trauma.

If you're reading with the intention of working to improve yourself, remember to occasionally put the book down as you experience "Wow, that's so true" moments and take the time to initiate dialogue with yourself. As you build character (good or bad), ponder how it affects the lives of people around you. Do you make life easier for someone by the way you think and express yourself, or do you hurt people with your actions and opinions? We must not be blind to our own shortcomings.

Life is tough. When you
see people underneath
the layers, the mask, and
the fear, make them feel
comfortable.

Try the following exercises. List three character strengths and at least one person in your life who benefits from them. How do they benefit? Jot down some ideas. Understanding how your character affects people around you will help you recognize the impact you already have on them.

For example:

1. Being Compassionate—My sister benefits from this the most. Whenever she's having a bad day, she calls me to vent and leans on me for advice.

Strength:
Person/People Affected:
How:

Strength:
Person/People Affected:
How:

Strength:
Person/People Affected:
How:

Now let's do the same with our weaknesses.

For example:

1. Impatience—My mother is affected by this the most. Sometimes when she's trying to give me advice or worrying about things I feel I already know, I dismiss her thoughts and talk over her, often saying, "I know, I know, Mom." I'm sure she gets irritated by that.

Weakness:
Person/People Affected:
How:

Weakness:
Person/People Affected:
How:

Weakness:
Person/People Affected:
How:

Self-awareness is gained through reflection.

Was it easy or difficult to point out your strengths and weaknesses? Are all of the weaknesses things you'd like to fix?

What action steps can you take to work on your weaknesses?

_____

_____

_____

Improving your character is challenging yet worth it. You only become wise, patient, kind, and forgiving with intention. Every day, you have the opportunity to work on yourself. Set daily goals and be honest with yourself so that you can recognize who you truly are and how you present yourself to the world.

Choose your character wisely. Your character often determines your legacy. As long as you're living, it's never too late to change the way you impact the world. Choose to be a good person—someone who makes life better for those around you.

No pressure. ☺

Chapter 9
Remedies and Takeaways:

- You are uniquely you.

- Paying attention to your motives and intentions will help you learn who you are.

- Be aware of the energy you give off. That energy is transferable to others.

- Make a list of your triggers (things that provoke you) and how you respond to them. Can you remove yourself from surroundings or people that trigger you in negative ways?

- How do you impact the lives of the people around you?

- Your character often determines your legacy.

CHAPTER 10

Level 10 Breakups and Crushes

"My worst heartbreak was my first girlfriend. We were together for three months and I was sure she was 'the one.' I didn't know that life goes on back then. I had never loved someone and been hurt like that. I didn't even know that I was gay at the time. That was in seventh grade."

—Curtis, Equinox receptionist and former foster child, age twenty-two

Dating as a teen is tough business. It's inevitable that at some point in your teen life you'll be rejected or experience heartbreak. Many parents ban their children from having boyfriends and girlfriends at a young age to prevent them from prematurely engaging in sexual behavior or to protect them from the intense emotions that occur when you really fall for someone. We all know that when you have a crush, that person absorbs much of your attention, and it's not easy to balance a relationship with friendships, extracurricular activities, and school.

A relationship is the way in which two or more people regard and behave toward each other.

The way people treat you in relationships depends on three things:
1. *How you allow them to treat you*
2. *Their past experiences*
3. *Their societal influences*

Have you ever heard the saying, "How a person treats you is a reflection of them, not you"? That's true, but how they continue to treat you is the result of what you allow and who they are as a result of their experiences. Take the relationship between a bully and a victim, for example. A bully torments the victim because of his or her own negative experiences and thoughts. At some point in the bully's life, they were taught this behavior, and although they probably know it's wrong, hurting someone else makes them feel better about themselves. However, the bully is only as powerful as their victim allows. As we discussed in chapter 4, the victim can take action to put an end to the bullying.

You should never allow yourself to continue to be a victim, especially when it comes to relationships. But how do you know if a relationship is healthy? As you start to date, you'll learn how to recognize and give love with time and experience. Making dating decisions is difficult when you're still trying to understand your own self-worth, but be patient with yourself and always honor your intuition. You may end up in a relationship with someone who is not as respectful and thoughtful as they should be, but you usually won't understand that until you give yourself the opportunity to date someone else and see that you were settling.

It's difficult to recognize what you haven't experienced. When a young girl has a father who is present, supportive, and caring, she will most likely grow up in search of a boyfriend who has similar traits. When you lack experience with healthy relationships, you might spend too much time in situations with people who aren't good for you. It's always best to take the time to get to know a person so you can understand who they are—and how they'll probably treat you—before deciding to date them. It's equally important to look at how you're treating people.

In order to experience love and learn what type of person complements you best, you'll have to deal with a breakup at some point. A breakup at your age may feel like the hardest thing you'll ever go through in life. You know—the end-of-the-world, Level 10 type of breakup.

Here's what qualifies as a Level 10 Breakup:

- You and a boyfriend/girlfriend who's also your classmate still have to see each other on a daily basis and breathe the same air for five days a week after you split—**that's about a Level 10 Breakup.**
- A crush who you're mentally preparing to date falls for someone else and act as if you were never an option—**that's a Level 10 (mental) Breakup.**
- A relationship that lasts at least two weeks and ends for any reason—**that's about a Level 10 Breakup.**
- Any relationship where you're emotionally invested and then have to explain to others why it didn't work out—**that's about a Level 10 Breakup.** (Who wants to explain anything to anyone when you

hardly understand it yourself?)

- Ending things with someone you thought you'd marry and spend the rest of your life with—**that's easily a Level 10 Breakup.**
- Someone who knows all of your deepest, darkest secrets leaving you—**that's definitely a Level 10 Breakup.**
- A boyfriend/girlfriend who causes a major argument and cancels out any chance of continuing a friendship once it's over—**that's a Level 10 Breakup.**

If it feels like a Level 10 Breakup, it is. Your feelings are real. Don't let anyone invalidate them.

Here's something you may not have discovered yet: once you make it through your first Level 10 Breakup, you live on!

#Level10BreakUp

So what's the recipe for finding comfort after a breakup?

- Reflect and be honest with yourself. Before you turn to your family and friends, you have to have a conversation with yourself, because you and your ex are the only ones who know the truth about the situation. What went wrong?
- Get back to yourself! What were you doing before your thoughts and time were consumed by someone else? This is your time to improve yourself, get more active, and build stronger relationships with your family and friends.
- Create. Express what you're feeling by making something new.
- Don't stalk! There is no point in trying to keep up with your ex. Looking at their social pages fifty times a day only slows down recovery.
- If there was anything left unsaid, write it down. Think about how you'd like to express your feelings in a mature manner, write it out, then sit with what you've written for a couple days. Would you have regrets if you never had the opportunity to share these words? Are you willing to share them knowing that you may not receive a response? If so, then get your thoughts off your chest. Call, say your message in person, or send a letter (electronic or paper). Then let go.

- Spend time alone and allow yourself to feel your honest thoughts and emotions. Sometimes when we keep ourselves too busy, we block our time to heal. Go home and cry. (My friends think I'm super strong and don't cry, but that's because I prefer not to cry in front of them. I cry my ugly tears at home in the comfort of my pajamas because that's what works for me.) Crying will help you relieve stress and tension.
- Have hope. You have to believe that there is someone out there in this humongous world who is compatible with you. Believe that you will meet them when you're finished healing and your heart is ready for more.
- Love yourself!

One day when I was about sixteen, I was arguing on the phone with my high school sweetheart and had no idea my father was in the hallway eavesdropping. I was crying because I'd found out my boyfriend had kissed another girl. I was devastated and wanted my boyfriend to feel my pain and fix things.

In the middle of the conversation, with my voice cracking as I swallowed salty tears, my father burst through the door, irate. "What are you crying for?" he said. "Nobody wants to sit around and listen to you cry! That's not going to make him like you more." In that moment, I paused and thought, *Okay, so not only do I have the worst boyfriend in the world, now I have the worst dad too!* I didn't realize that my father was just trying to toughen me up and protect me. Crying is what I had always done when suffering from pain, but ever since that day, I find myself thinking about whether or not the person is really worth my tears.

Communication

Just because you speak to someone daily on social media or check in with short text messages doesn't mean you have a strong bond or really know that person well. **Don't confuse consistent communication with meaningful conversation.** Sometimes checking in with someone is simply the minimal effort needed to keep that person interested.

Instead, take the time to meet in person and *really* talk. Get your head out of your phone and practice making conversation eye-to-eye. Investing in a serious relationship with someone requires learning each other's interests, goals, and fears. When you talk in person about these things, there's no room for misinterpretation because you can see and feel the emotion behind the words. Be sure to communicate when something is bothering you too. Part of building a healthy relationship involves talking out your differences or expressing when you feel hurt, wronged, or jealous.

Jealousy Is Not a Compliment

If your crush or significant other got an opportunity that placed them with new or attractive people, would you be happy for them or threatened by the thought that maybe they'd develop feelings for someone else? Maybe you'd feel a little bit of both . . .

Experiencing jealousy is normal. However, projecting jealous feelings onto others is not okay. Jealousy is an uncomfortable feeling that stems from personal insecurities, fears, and your personal experience. Sometimes these feelings arise from assumptions or things that aren't real. This emotion tells us a lot about ourselves and others. Pay close attention to your inner thoughts when you experience jealousy. Are they selfish or justified? Selfish thoughts won't get you anywhere.

People are not property that you own or control for the betterment of your world. Jealousy can create an imbalance of power, and dangerous situations can develop. To reject this type of behavior, respectful communication must take place. Communication will help both parties better understand each other and how their actions reflect their maturity and readiness to be in a relationship. If you or your partner are experiencing feelings of jealousy that lead to unhealthy actions or decisions, then you're not equipped to be together (for now).

Check yourself. Refer back to chapter 3 for help with quieting your mind. A good partner will support the other person's personal choices, respect them, and give them space. These are all gestures that you should prioritize in order to build a healthy relationship.

What Is a Healthy Relationship?
Fill in the blanks with traits that you feel represent each side.

Healthy Relationship Characteristics

(e.g. Respect, Support . . .)

Unhealthy Relationship Characteristics

(e.g. Mistrust, Manipulation . . .)

_____   _____

_____   _____

_____   _____

_____   _____

_____   _____

_____   _____

_____   _____

_____   _____

_____   _____

Self-comfort is not just coaching yourself through pain. It's also recognizing who or what caused it and how you can prevent yourself from being in that type of situation again.

Life is hard. We have absolutely no idea what and who is meant to be in our lives forever. Some of us don't even know our sexual preferences. You have to be patient and just stay true to yourself in order to attract what's best for you.

I went to a psychic when I was twenty, and she confirmed that my first boyfriend would be "the one." Well, she was wrong. He now has three children, and I'm not their mother. I really did think he was the one. We dated throughout high school and helped each other grow through our very honest friendship, but . . . we could not predict the future and we grew apart.

People come and go, and everyone who enters your life will be there for a season or a reason. Your experiences make you stronger and the lessons are yours to learn. Don't try to do what everyone else is doing if it doesn't feel right. People around you will "serial date," hook up, get serious, or stay away from dating altogether. There are distractions that come with dating and emotional feelings that not everyone can manage. Whatever you're focused on, just remember that whatever is meant for you will be yours; you should never have to fight for the attention or affection of anyone. If they're not giving you what you want, it's because they don't want to or you're incompatible. You deserve better.

Remember: Don't rely on something outside of yourself to feel good; that will make you live a life of dependency that holds you back from loving and living at your greatest potential.

The first person you should worry about dating is yourself. How well do you know yourself? Is it enough to comfortably explain your wants and needs to others? Unless you know yourself, you won't understand how you should be treated by others.

The best relationships blossom from friendship with someone who truly has your best interests at heart. It is possible to meet your soulmate in your teen years, but take your time, discover who you truly are, and wait until after college before you make that final decision to stay together. After all, you're still changing and your needs will change too.

Don't force love. Even
if it means feeling lonely
sometimes.

Chapter 10
Remedies and Takeaways:

- Life is hard enough trying to learn to love yourself; adding someone else to the equation makes it even harder.

- Everything you feel is real.

- The love you look for is often what you've been taught by those around you.

- A breakup is not the end of the world—even though it feels like it.

- People are not property that you can control.

- If you can't communicate, you can't relationship!

- You can't force someone to have feelings for you that aren't there. You have to accept that and set them free of your expectations.

CHAPTER 11

Thinking Beyond Transition

"People always say 'I don't want to do this' or 'I don't want to be here,' but they don't focus on where they want to go. You can't go to a travel agent to book a trip, name all the places you don't want to go, and expect them to figure out the best destination for you."
—Jovian Zayne, certified coach and founder,
The OnPurpose Movement

#MovingOn

This chapter is for youth living in transition or for those who know others who are going through it. Transition can mean living in temporary housing or foster care, going to a new school, or moving into a new home, town, or state. It's all temporary but so difficult to face. There's no pain like being ripped out of your home with a trash bag or finding out you have no place to sleep. There are levels of transition that mentally crush youth because they're not prepared and don't know how to cope.

Most kids move at least once during their childhood, but foster children move approximately twice a year. It can be a very traumatic experience when you have no say in where you're going.

One time I met a young girl who was living in a homeless shelter because her family was the victim of a house fire—an intentional fire set by local gang members that forced the family to run to the top level of their home and jump out an attic window. The young girl, who once lived a stable life, learned very quickly that everything can be taken away in an instant. After losing their home, her family was placed in a local shelter. The girl was fully aware of what had happened and decided she was going to stay positive and optimistic while her parents saved to move into a new home.

Most children feel shame in living in transition, but this particular young girl knew that transition was temporary and held onto the possibility of having stability again. She volunteered to share her story at a Precious Dreams Foundation Comfort Drop, hoping to help other teens feel like they weren't alone. She understood their pain and wanted to give them strength and hope. Most teens are not brave enough to share their stories, but sharing is a way to release negative emotions associated with life-changing experiences.

Being in transition can create a range of emotions—from anger and resentment to fear, anxiety, and sadness. Dealing with these emotions can make life even harder, especially when it comes to building relationships in school. Moving can shake up your entire world, and sometimes parents don't understand how hard that can be. As a minor, you don't have the power to live where you'd like, but you do have the power to self-comfort and do things that inspire a positive frame of mind.

If given advance notice, you can plan to do things like pack comfort items and notify friends in hopes of maintaining relationships. Thanks to technology, you can call, text, or use parent-approved social media to stay in touch with old friends or connect to play games online. If you move, I challenge you to try staying in touch with friends. If you form a strong enough bond, these people will help you as you move from place to place even in your adulthood. A person doesn't have to be physically present to provide comfort and give you a sense of home.

Have you ever thought about the options you have for living somewhere new in your adulthood? Maybe this is a place you'd like to experience after high school or college. List three places that you could see yourself living one day (all at least five miles away from your current neighborhood).

_____

_____

_____

Frequent moves can be emotionally draining and downright difficult, but I've witnessed some positive outcomes from friends who grew up in foster care and experienced many placements. People who move often learn how to better cope with change, which helps teens become more flexible and adaptable when dealing with surprise occurrences and new beginnings.

Being in transition at a young age has helped kids prepare for going off to college or moving for future work, where everything is new and unknown. What will seem like instability at times is preparing you for great things ahead.

The people who are destined to be in your life will always find their way back to you. You may lose friends with your absence, but that's okay. Learn how to build relationships with people who share your interests and value the connection you share, even between the times when you see each other. Adult friendships are based on an equal effort to stay in touch and make plans, because adult friends don't have the luxury of seeing each other every day at school or at sports practice.

Adjustment Strategies

If you have difficulty adjusting to new environments, try some of these tips:

Get to know your school counselor. Don't take for granted the opportunity to get to know your school counselor. Counselors can be a great resource and source of support if you open up to them about your issues and needs. The more information they have, the more help they can provide.

Find a mentor. A mentor is someone who believes in you, motivates you, and offers advice. Benefits of a healthy relationship with a mentor can include tutoring and life skills training. They can help you decrease negative behaviors and inspire you to make progress toward your dreams. These are the type of people who will feed your soul with everything it needs to boost your confidence.

Be yourself. As you go into new environments, don't try to adapt to how everyone else is acting. The real friends are the ones who like you for who you are. Don't get off on the wrong foot by playing pretend. If you lie about who you are, you'll eventually be found out. Be authentic and save yourself the trouble.

Make the first move. Opportunities are missed every day by people who are simply afraid to say hello. Make eye contact, hold your head high, and walk with confidence among your peers. Your presence in every new environment is a gift to those around you. Invite other teens to approach you by giving someone a smile or a compliment. If that doesn't work, there's always the classic "Do you have Instagram?" which can lead to a social media connection where people can get to know you through the images you share.

Try this exercise:
Put the book down for a second and count every blue item you see in the room.

Now that you have that number, can you tell me how many red items you saw? I'm sure you can't tell me without looking back, because you were only focused on the blue.

You must think beyond transition. You might feel stuck in today, but these twenty-four hours will pass, and you have the rest of your life in front of you. Focus on your interests and dreams, not on the things out of your control. Don't give up hope.

I know there's a lot of pressure to have everything figured out. Adults usually start asking children, "What do you want to be when you grow up?" as soon as they can understand the question. Growing up is scary enough without the pressure and expectations to impress the world, and those pressures seem even more overwhelming if you're in transition. It's hard to figure out where you'll go to college or what city or country you'd like to live in when you're always bouncing around from place to place. But the big picture is important. Do your best to stay focused on your future.

You truly are the author of your own story (although you may have to share writing credit with the people raising you). When you think of your future, it is you who plans and executes your life's middle and ending. The world is full of limitless possibilities for fun, fearless individuals—and don't believe anyone who tells you otherwise.

Spend more time counting your blessings. There is always someone with less. A big part of self-comfort is talking yourself through what's stress-worthy and setting limits on how long you should focus on the things you can't change. Allow your new environment to teach you something and focus on the bright side of things.

If your current transitional housing does not feel safe, say something! If you're in foster care, report the issue to someone at the agency, and if you're in a situation where you're afraid of getting in trouble, suggest someone pay a visit so they can see and learn about the current situation firsthand. Then the complaint doesn't trace back to you.

Chapter 11
Remedies and Takeaways:

- Being in transition is temporary. Don't get complacent here.

- Home is not a place you can see. It's only something you can feel.

- Much like living in transition, you'll learn that life will often lead you to many new places and unexpected turns

- Embrace change. Those who adapt well do well.

- If you can't change it, make it work.

CHAPTER 12

Instant Comfort Tools

"I think journaling was more like an itch that had to be scratched. I was angry as a kid and didn't know what I was angry about half of the time, but writing set me free in a way like nothing else. It was my peaceful escape."

—Gigi Blanchard,
writer, teacher, and former juvenile prisoner

Journey to Journaling

My friend Gigi Blanchard and I bonded while volunteering for Precious Dreams Foundation, but we quickly discovered that we had even more in common than a strong desire to give back. For both of us, journaling played a huge role in our youth and helped save us from ourselves. Although we have quite a bit in common, we had extremely different upbringings. Gigi was from Illinois, where she spent her teen years in and out of group homes. She was a good girl at heart, but she felt so lost and lonely that she looked for outlets outside of her home to dump her frustrations. At fifteen, she ended up stealing a car and was sentenced to a juvenile prison. Just like that, her freedom was taken. She was sent away for six years.

During her time in transition, Gigi credits most of her comfort and coping to writing:

> In my teens, I didn't trust anybody and I didn't understand my own feelings. Writing was my way of figuring it out. I would write out my thoughts or letters to people I didn't know if I would ever see again, like my mom; I had things I wanted to say to her and needed to get out. Writing is one thing that, no matter where I got sent or what else they took from me, could not be taken away.

Journaling is one of the best ways to self-comfort and unwind. They say if you jot ideas down before you go to sleep, you'll be less likely to stay awake worrying or stressing about them. There are no rules to journaling. You can write ideas, poetry, goals, music, stories, messages to God, or anything else you want. These are your private words, meant for your eyes only.

Expressing your unfiltered emotions gives you the authority and freedom to write your own story. Reflecting on what you've written and taking the time to analyze and understand your emotions will give you more control over your future narrative. Start by writing down the basics:

Dear _____

Today I feel _____

Today I learned _____

It bothers me when _____

I wish _____

Write out your thoughts, whether they are good or bad. It's a way to transfer your concerns and fears onto paper. Writing can also help you record important memories and emotions. Reading your old writing is better than looking at a photograph. Looking back on all you've overcome can bring comfort. (Keep your journal in a private place so it doesn't get read by a sibling or parent. We all know people can be nosey and may discover things we've written that we don't want them to see. Be careful.)

Meditation and Yoga

Finding comfort in school gets harder as your number of teachers increases. It's nearly impossible to build a substantial relationship with all of your teachers in an environment where you see them for short periods of time. You shuffle from place to place with the sound of a bell, leaving little time for anything outside of learning. Your brain is fed information period after period. Even between classes, you're surrounded by people and more information to ingest.

Today's average teen is overstimulated and keeps a busy calendar. When you are constantly looking down at a phone, reading, participating in extracurricular activities, keeping up on the latest news, or tackling school and family issues, there isn't much time to dedicate to your thoughts. There isn't much time to calm them either.

Meditation is a mindfulness practice that helps us focus on the most important thing: what's right in front of us. The first time I meditated, I realized that my room was a mess. It was my first experience using the Insight Timer app, which instructed me to open my eyes and look around. When I followed the instructions, I was completely shocked by the mess surrounding me. All the rushing around I'd been doing caused a pile-up of clothes everywhere. I had even been sleeping with clothes on my bed and hardly noticed. In that moment, I struggled with calming my thoughts, but I told myself to focus and get to cleaning after I finished meditating. My mind needed cleaning before my room!

Meditation is more than sitting still or playing the quiet game. It's the practice of being one with your mind. It has no rules, time limits, or mandatory sitting positions. Everyone has their own unique way of focusing on breath and connecting to source energy, and you're bound to find *something* among the hundreds of different forms of meditation that will work for you. Although the most popular position is sitting (Sukhasana), many people take long walks (sans cell phones) or simply go outside to feel the grass and clear their minds.

If taken seriously, yoga and meditation can be one of the most effective ways to self-comfort. Meditation can push out toxic and unnecessary thoughts. It has also been shown to create positive results in high school students and enhance focus for children with ADHD. During the school season, you're constantly working on deadlines: to finish papers, complete homework, or finish tests within the time limit. From roughly eight in the morning until three in the afternoon every day, you're inundated with a mass of new information. With this flood of new knowledge, tight deadlines, and the pressure to succeed, it's no wonder so many kids become anxious.

Meditation helps you appreciate the silence that can be created even in the noisiest of environments.

#QuickRelease

Try this meditation exercise:

- Lie down on a flat surface and close your eyes. Take deep breaths and feel the support of the ground beneath you. Focus on your breath and how the air moves through your body.
- With your eyes closed, place your hands on your heart and visualize yourself in a space that gives you optimal peace.

- For the next three minutes, focus on the joy and gratitude that emerge from your visualization.
- Breathing deeply in and out, turn off any distracting thoughts and allow yourself to stay in this emotional state of appreciation.

Were you able to get through the entire practice with no inner or outer interruption? If not, don't feel discouraged. It is called a "practice" for a reason. You can try dimming the lights or lighting a candle to give you some assistance next time. Once you can get through meditation successfully, you'll begin to see how it benefits you throughout the day.

During one Comfort Drop at a shelter in Queens, Precious Dreams Foundation collaborated with the Urban Yogis to show homeless teens how to practice yoga and meditation. The Urban Yogis are part of the Peace Is a Lifestyle program, which consists of five young adults from the south side of Queens who have all been personally affected by gun violence. The guys teach free yoga and meditation in inner cities to give positive options to kids who hang out on the streets. While most teens at the Comfort Drop were hesitant to relax and focus, some were 100 percent committed from beginning to end. You might find a natural love for yoga, learning to enjoy it with time and practice, or you may discover that you prefer other comfort methods instead.

Practicing yoga has many benefits. It's a time to let everything go and reconnect with yourself. In the beginning, it may seem difficult moving your body in unfamiliar ways, but with practice there are many rewards. Through yoga, you'll build muscle, flexibility, and peace of mind. You'll also learn to trust yourself more.

Since I struggle with ADHD, meditation is difficult for me. I've found that simply counting my breaths or practicing yoga helps me quiet my mind, and it's become my personal preference for comfort. It reminds me of the feelings I get when I'm dancing, except there's no sound. Yoga is something you can do in any open space at any time of the day because it only requires you and your body for participation. It will help you sleep better, think positively about your body image, and feel more optimistic.

Find out if yoga or meditation will work for you. There are plenty of free resources to help you get started. Try searching the web for free videos or picking up a book from your local library.

Other Options
Besides journaling, yoga, and meditation, there are plenty of other ways you can find instant comfort. You might find your healthy release through playing a sport, going to church, practicing a musical instrument, going for a walk, listening to music, dancing, drawing, painting, sewing, gaming, daydreaming, reading, cooking, watching a movie, taking a shower, taking a nap, or any number of other methods.

Challenge yourself to pick a comfort mechanism and practice it for the next thirty days. Carve out at least two hours a week to do this specific activity and evaluate how it makes you feel. If you notice a difference in your mood, stick with it or add another mechanism to your calendar. In the end, practicing self-comfort will help you gain the balance needed to reduce stress.

The tension you feel in your mind is probably affecting the rest of your body as well. We've all rubbed our foreheads, messed with our nails, or tapped our foot during anxious or stressful times. Find comfort in your skin and let your own touch calm you. Sometimes when I give a speech, I rub my hands together or move them around a lot, the same way I would if I were cold. You could also try reaching back and giving yourself a good ol' one-handed shoulder massage. Figure out what works for you, and find instant comfort methods that help instead of harm.

Activity:

Illustrate everything that makes you happy—this could include people, places, activities, or things. Draw them scattered around the next couple of pages; when you're finished, fold the top corner of the page. This book and these two pages will be your instant comfort-tool master list. In times of emergency, pick up the book, go to those pages, and focus on the good.

Chapter 12
Remedies and Takeaways:

- Never underestimate the power of releasing your feelings by writing them out.

- There are no rules to journaling.

- The vulnerability that's expressed in your writing must be protected. Place your notebook or journal in a safe place at all times.

- Try meditation. Meditation provides a sense of calm confidence and can push out toxic and unnecessary thoughts.

- Do you know how good it feels to stretch?

- Focus on your master list. When you're angry, think about the things that help you get out of that space.

- There are many ways to release. You just have to find the one that works best for you. Is it music, art, reading, dance, sports, school? Go where there is comfort.

CHAPTER 13

Have You Ever Lost Somebody?

"How do I comfort myself when I'm grieving?" was the question my eighteen-year-old cousin asked me when she lost her father to cancer.

Everything living will die at some point, and that thought is a heavy one to bear.

I remember being in total shock when I received a call that my uncle had passed away. Not only was I unprepared for his passing, but I had no idea he had been battling cancer for almost a year. I felt instant heartbreak. I was devastated. My feelings went from shock to sadness and then to regret that I didn't get to say goodbye and spend more time with him. Now that I look back, I don't even know if saying goodbye would've made things any easier.

There's nothing that makes a teen feel more alone than the loss of someone who is very close to them. People will say everything possible to express their condolences, but it's never enough. No one can understand the connection you've now lost.

Mourn your loss with no deadline.

When you experience great loss, you might not deal with the emotion until months or even years later. In some cases, people will be in denial and feel empty or out of sorts until they're able to understand and accept that death means no return.

A person who passes away is gone in physical form. Some people feel that spirits live on; others believe they become angels. And some believe that people just live on in our memories. Whatever you believe, always remember that love does not die. Let your loved ones live in your heart forever. If you feel the urge to speak to them, try writing a letter or talking to them out loud. There is no evidence that they're completely gone. What happens after death has never been proven.

#LoveNeverLeavesItsInsideOfYou

The loss of a friend or close family member can affect grades, appetite, relationships, or mental health. We can be hard on ourselves because we feel guilty or angry, but are those emotions honoring the person who died? Would they want you to feel that way? If their spirit were present, would they approve of the decisions you're making? Honor the deceased through your actions; showcase what you've learned from the positive and negative aspects of their life.

Has the death of someone you didn't even know affected you? Sometimes we grieve over parents or family members who passed before we could build a relationship with them. Some children are forced to grieve over the absence of a parent who is living but may be in jail or the military. It all hurts, but you have to think about it, feel it, and talk yourself through it in order to be okay. You are the only presence you need to survive.

Denial delays recovery.

Grieving does not make you weak—it makes you better. Speak your pain and release your hurt. It's okay to cry (ugly tears) and grieve. The times that I make the most use of my journal are when I'm suffering. My journal has been my safe place and has allowed me to release the heartbreak.

Write a letter to someone who has passed away or is absent in your life. Tell them something you never got to say or share a way they've influenced you to be the person you are today.

Dear _____,

I yearn to heal.
I yearn to feel.
I need love.

Talking about your loss is a source of healing and helps release pain.

Ask yourself:

- Would the person who passed away want you to suffer forever because of their loss?
- How would they want you to move forward in their memory? How can you make them proud?
- What would make them smile?
- How can you continue their legacy?

Providing Compassion to Others

If you know someone who is grieving, it's hard to figure out how to help them. Everyone grieves in their own way, and you don't have the power to make everything better again, but you can be supportive. Ask them sensitive questions and allow them to vent or even cry. Create a relationship where your friend knows they can be open and vulnerable with you without judgment, and assure them that you won't share what they say with others. If they don't feel like opening up, tell them you'll be there for them when they're ready. Don't invade the space they require or rush the process. Just give them love.

Grieving over Lost Relationships

Sometimes you lose someone who is still alive. You might simply drift apart from that person as you both grow and change. The person you confided in the most and shared your best moments with is sometimes the person who will leave you without warning. This person was a temporary companion. You can understand their purpose by reflecting on the times you had together and why they came to an end. Perhaps this person has moved away, or you did something hurtful to them and they've decided to block you from their life. Maybe it ended in a way that will teach one or both of you how not to treat others.

Let go and grow. A relationship that's meant to be doesn't have to be forced.

Life won't be what you imagined, but it'll pan out the way it should. It will always surprise you, and although we can plan and prepare, there are many things that are simply out of our control. Stay open to what comes and what goes. It's all happening for a reason.

Chapter 13
Remedies and Takeaways:

- Mourn. You have to release the anger and sadness that follow.

- It's okay to spend some time in solitude.

- Mourn your loss with no deadline, but remember that mourning should feel like a release. Do not take on unnecessary feelings or guilt.

- Use very considerate words when talking to someone who has lost a loved one. If you don't know what to say, just let them know you're there to support them. Sometimes just being present speaks volumes.

- Don't invade the space of someone who is mourning, don't rush the process, and just give them love.

- What is meant to be is happening right now.

- The past is the past, and it's useless to focus on things you can't change.

CHAPTER 14

Anger Issues, Anyone?!

"I remember one day a kid flicked my ear and I just lost it on him. All of the anger I built up inside for my parents not being around came out in that moment, and I was just hitting him because I was hurting. That was the day I realized I needed help. I didn't want to hurt people."

—Jason Humble,
entrepreneur and former foster child

One of the hardest emotions to deal with is anger. Anger feels like a fireball running through your veins, making it hard to control your mind and body. The fire wants to erupt, and sometimes letting it out feels better than keeping it in. However, like fire, anger can be a destructive thing if not controlled.

There are many examples of situations and disappointments that create understandable rage. **You always and absolutely have a right to feel angry,** but when you get dangerously upset, you have to remember **you have the power to control your anger** because it's a feeling that's triggered by your thoughts. Don't do things that'll make the situation worse.

Oftentimes when we're angry, we create chaos. Angry people can hurt themselves and others by acting out in ways that are detrimental to their surroundings. Shouting, breaking things, acting out of revenge, damaging someone's personal belongings, using hurtful words, or making rash decisions—these actions can all have damaging effects. Instead of lashing out, channel your anger into something positive.

Entrepreneur Jason Humble shared his story with Precious Dreams Foundation, revealing that he didn't understand how to control his anger issues in high school. He found himself always getting into fights and feeling the need to physically defend himself against anything he took personally. Jason felt like he couldn't confide in anyone at the time; it was the recommendation to see a therapist and develop a relationship with God that changed his life. As a teen, praying to a higher power provided the guidance and direction that Jason yearned for. Today, Jason leans on his faith and his relationships with supportive friends and his foster parents to feel positive.

Unfortunately, in most scenarios when someone acts out of anger, they get punished or reprimanded. People aren't usually looking to help the angry person (that's a bigger issue with society that we can save for another book). This makes the situation more frustrating for the person who was acting out. It takes the mind from a place of anger to disappointment in oneself or others. Don't count on others to rescue you from your anger. Take the initiative to work on managing your anger in a healthy way.

I know, I know. Easier said than done. Anger is one of those things that seem to slip out. Have you ever found yourself saying or wishing things that you didn't mean? Have you ever wished harm on someone you love (maybe a sibling or parent) because they upset you and you were reacting without thinking? It's crazy how anger can consume you and make you forget all the good in your world. Hurtful words are not cool, and once they're spoken they can't be unsaid.

Maybe you're not angry. Perhaps you're just passionate.

Pay Attention to Yourself

There are a few tips you can learn to calm yourself when in a state of anger and react in a reasonable and intelligent manner. As you're learning, self-comfort isn't solely the act of making yourself feel good. It's also about learning to calm your thoughts. When you find yourself doing things that feel wrong, use a neutral tone of voice to cut in and ask what you're doing. It helps to take a step back and think about your actions whenever you feel your control slipping. Stop and use your head.

There are signals that often go unnoticed when the body is building up anger. You might start breathing harder or your hands might get tense. As you feel tension growing, become more conscious of yourself than you are of what's in front of you. This is the moment that you can begin telling yourself to stay calm and not say anything you'll regret. Your conversation with yourself is more important than what can be said to anyone else in a time of anger. For example: "I won't let this upset me. This teacher is being unfair, but I need to calm down because I can't win by arguing with her. I need to show the facts to my parents or my principal and let them handle it. If I argue with an adult, that can affect my grade and make matters worse."

Go Sweat

Most people don't work out for psychological and emotional benefits, but they should! Working out decreases tension and can keep you mentally and physically fit. It can also boost self-esteem and give you a clearer complexion.

Research shows that teens who don't exercise will keep that pattern throughout their whole lives. If you aren't being physically active, you can change that by taking small steps. Start with planks or a ten-minute walk every day and download an app to count your steps. You can compete with your daily goal and slowly increase your steps each day.

Create a Safe Page

A safe page is a piece of paper you can use to write out every angry thought and get them off your chest. Say all the things you *feel*, but don't necessarily *mean*. Get everything out. Then rip the paper into a gazillion pieces and let it go. The page is safe because it will never be seen and you're the only one who knows what you expressed in the moment.

Turn to Music

Music is an effective stress-management tool. Sometimes it helps to simply listen to lyrics written by someone who has dealt with a similar situation or to hear a song that will help you visualize a completely different scenario from the one you currently inhabit. Music provides an instant comfort and helps you understand that your feelings are normal and you're not alone.

- When you're feeling angry, grab some headphones.
- When you're traveling to a place that makes you anxious, find a song for the ride.
- When you need a boost of positive energy, put on the feel-good song that gets you going.

Choose Uplifting, Supportive Friends

Friends should never do harmful things to you on purpose or make you feel bothered. If this happens, be sure to communicate with others about how their actions make you feel. Or, if their anger-inducing behavior is part of a trend, channel that anger to create a protective barrier around yourself and start avoiding these harmful individuals and situations. Use your anger to guide and protect you instead of stooping to the level of those who are provoking or teasing you.

Dealing with Triggers

We all have triggers that can set us off or take us out of character. Become aware of what triggers your anger so you can begin figuring out how it affects you. Learn how to solve conflict by communicating the issue. If you're too angry to express yourself in the moment, give yourself time and revisit the issue when you're ready. You have the right to share with others how their behavior or decisions affect you.

#FightingWords

Words resonate deeper
when they're expressed
maturely.

Some of our greatest leaders took their pain and frustration and communicated them in impressive ways. Are you familiar with the actions of Martin Luther King, Jr. or Mahatma Gandhi? Do you know about the nonviolent resistance of the Montgomery Bus Boycott, the National American Woman Suffrage Association, or the more recent Women's March? There's much to learn about inner strength and confidence from these leaders and groups who stood together to advocate for their beliefs. As Gandhi said, "Nonviolence is an intensely active force when properly understood and used."

We get positive results from behaving in a rational and peaceful manner. It's been proven for years and is extremely difficult to master, but it can be achieved with practice. For many years, as black people in America were stoned, taunted, and abused, they focused on boycotting and fighting back through protest to gain the rights and respect they deserved. When you communicate intelligently and calmly, it helps to solve the issue.

If these tips are too challenging or don't seem to work, it may be time to ask for help. Don't be embarrassed to admit that you're struggling with managing your anger and would like assistance. Set up a meeting with your school counselor and share your issues.

It's time to find your zen. Protect your peace and create barriers.

Chapter 14
Remedies and Takeaways:

- Angry reactions can cause long-term negative effects and damage.

- There is a lesson to be learned from every experience that provokes your anger.

- Yelling does not force people to understand your words better. It's simply a volume change.

- Take note of your triggers and make necessary changes to remove yourself from people and situations that promote negative thoughts and reactions.

- Behaving in a peaceful and rational manner always produces better results.

CHAPTER 15

Protect Yourself

"The first time I had sex, I was only fourteen years old and it was because of peer pressure. Every time after that, I was just chasing a thrill. I wish I knew back then that you find love through connection."

—Ro James, R&B artist

This chapter is about sex, sexual feelings, inappropriate physical behavior, and everything that relates to protecting your body.

How do you know when you're ready to explore your body boundaries and learn what you like or don't want? Only you can answer that question. Body boundaries are your personal set of rules for how and when people should touch you. When you're feeling ready to explore your urges, don't just jump in feet-first. Be sure to educate yourself as much as possible. Unfortunately, you can't erase or take back intimate experiences with others, so you have to be careful with each and every decision.

Kissing, touching, and sexual intercourse may be difficult topics to discuss with parents. If you have a trusted adult with whom you can discuss some of these topics, great! You're one of the lucky few. If not, use reliable sources on the internet or in the library to educate yourself as much as possible. Among other topics to research, it's important to think about the potential consequences of sexual activity. For example:

- How much do you know about STIs (sexually transmitted infections)?
- Did you know that you can get herpes from kissing? Do you understand the harmful effects of STIs?
- Did you know that young people between the ages of fifteen and twenty-four account for 50 percent of all new STIs, although they represent just 25 percent of the sexually experienced population?

#ProtectYourself

People don't look like they have STIs. That status isn't public, and sometimes the person with the infection doesn't even know they're carrying it. Since teens often find discomfort in sharing with adults that they're sexually active, they don't get regularly tested. Many STIs don't have visual or physical symptoms, so a teen may think they're in the clear when they're not. When people don't protect themselves, they are at risk for contracting whatever infections their partner has from their previous sexual interactions. They also risk teen pregnancy.

You will have sexual feelings before you're ready to have sex.

How do you know if the other person is ready? Ask them. If you don't receive verbal consent, then you shouldn't assume touching in a sexual manner is consensual. If you're not comfortable enough to have the conversation, you're definitely not ready for sex.

Saying "no" isn't easy, but not saying it can leave you full of regret. You have to trust yourself enough to know when it's the right time for you. If it's not the right time, use your voice, hands, feet, or any other means necessary to say no. If you're in a situation where the person blames you for getting them aroused and asks you to help them "get off" or "take care of them," stand your ground and stick with your no. You don't owe anybody anything. You are only in control of your body.

How do you know you're ready for something that you've never done before? You don't. However, you know if things make you feel uncomfortable, those are signs that you should not ignore. Your timing shouldn't be compared to what anybody around you is doing. If alcohol, drugs, or peer pressure are involved, that's even more reason to say no. You don't want to make permanent decisions when you're not in a normal state of mind!

Words to Live By:

Don't hold on to a person who does not have your best interest at heart only because you want their love.

Having sex with someone is not a good strategy for making them like you.

Someone who loves you will not make threats. Someone who loves you will not intentionally make you cry. Someone who cares about you will not pressure you to feel uncomfortable.

Don't become numb to something or accept what doesn't create peace in your heart.

"NO SEXT
IS
SAFE SEXT"

One in five teens admits to sexting (sending explicit photos or text via private message). This is another area where you should be sure about what you're ready for and aware of the risks. There's an assumption that what's being sent will remain private; however, there's no guarantee that it will. You own your body and you own your photos, but once you share either of the two, you give up a lot of your power. And even if you trust the person you send a sext to, there's always the chance that their data could be exposed to someone with malicious intent. Share what you want with people, not their devices.

Emotional Abuse
We live in a world of imperfect people. My hope for everyone reading this is that you'll never be placed in a situation where you can't protect yourself, but unfortunately it happens. If you have experienced physical abuse, emotional abuse, sexual abuse, or neglect, there's never a bad time to speak up!

Emotional abuse does mental damage and is equally as violent as physical abuse. If someone calls you names, tries to embarrass you, doesn't allow you to make decisions, invalidates your opinions, threatens you, isolates you, belittles your aspirations, or does bad things and then blames you for their behavior, they are practicing a form of emotional abuse. Damage from emotional abuse can't be reversed. You don't deserve this type of treatment—it's not normal and should not be tolerated.

Another serious social issue is sexual harassment.

Sexual harassment is harassment in a workplace or any other professional or social situation that involves unwanted sexual advances or obscene remarks.

Inappropriate words and gestures are also harassment. If you're experiencing sexual harassment, document the behavior and share it with someone who has the authority to help. This new world will not tolerate old ways. There are even ways you can report things anonymously to protect your safety. When you reach out for help, ask for your options in order to make yourself feel comfortable enough to tell everything!

There are dangerous people lurking all around trying to take advantage of us in hurtful, inappropriate, and harmful ways. Broken people may cut down others in their pursuit to put their own pieces back together. Even if you love the abuser or they're someone in a position of authority, it's never okay to let someone take away your self-esteem or force you to do anything you don't want to do. No one deserves to be abused. Listen to your mind on this one. If you know it's wrong, it's wrong—and there's nothing a person can say or do to justify that.

Speak up if someone ever tries to emotionally or physically harm you, and don't be afraid to save yourself! By law, your school officials have to file a report to protect you if you tell them something harmful is happening to you. If nothing is done, tell someone else. Continue to speak up until the problem is rectified. Never feel like your voice should be silenced if you share with an adult who doesn't help you. It may be that the person you confided in just doesn't know the right thing to do. Continue to speak out until you're heard and something is done in your favor.

You'll only be defeated by the things you refuse to fight.

Speak up to someone you trust and be truthful about everything you say. Protecting yourself is empowering. Protect the truth. Protect what's real. Being your own hero can sometimes save others.

Self-Comfort Rule: Stay clear of people who don't respect that your mind and body belong to you.

Chapter 15
Remedies and Takeaways:

- Your body, your decision.

- If it doesn't feel right, then it's not.

- No sexting is safe sexting.

- Abuse in all forms should not be tolerated.

- Protect yourself from sexual harassment. Speak up and take necessary actions to do what's right.

CHAPTER 16

The Outlook—Advancing Through Adversity

"The harder you work when nobody is watching, the less you'll struggle when it's time to perform and do what you need to do in life."

—Brandon Jennings, NBA player
and Precious Dreams Foundation guest speaker

Do you ever feel like bad things always happen to you and nothing ever goes your way? Is it hard to see the relationship between cause and effect? Do you watch unfortunate circumstances unfold in front of you and feel like a victim? All of these thoughts are common, but they don't have to be constant.

We're all born into different circumstances, similar to the first round of cards in a poker game. Everyone starts off with the hand that was given to them. So what happens when you're dealt a bad hand?

When life deals you a bad hand, how do you react?

1. Sulk and complain. Play the game while pouting and thinking you don't have a chance of winning.
2. Throw your cards in and give up before you even start playing.
3. Pretend your cards are good to try to convince others that you're competition and hope your confidence will mess up their game.
4. Play the round hoping to win.
5. Impatiently wait for the game to be over so you can get new cards and try again.

In life, you're guaranteed to lose many times. However, how you react to situations will determine if you get more chances to win when you lose. What will be your poker face as you take those L's?

You are guaranteed to face disappointment. You will fail and fall hard. These are things that are promised for everyone, no matter the color of your skin, financial status, or current circumstances. So how will you play the game of life?

Here are some tips for those who want to give up:

Immediately focus on your options.
Asking for new cards is not an option. Similarly, if we could pick our physical appearance (like one of those build-a-character apps) we would, but we simply can't. Your unique appearance is the hand you were dealt, and the way you groom and dress is how you play it. When the cards are dealt, you must use your skills and ingenuity to get the best results. Which cards can you use for your benefit? You'll only learn to win when you study the game and get better at playing it.

Bluff, bluff, bluff.
Remember how well Beyoncé kept her composure while dealing with her relationship challenges (before the world saw her bust the car windows open in the *Lemonade* video)? You don't have to share your hand with anyone. People expect you to lose when you act defeated. Celebrities have their best mental breakdowns at home with their families and therapists. You can too! Put your shoulders back, keep your head up, and speak and act with confidence no matter what. When you're dealing with hardships, it gets harder to have everyone else's opinions or negative thoughts in the mix too. You can't win when the nonbelievers are making the most noise.

Celebrate the win even if it's not yours.

So you didn't get the results you expected. That's okay! Your win might be in the next hand. How much support do you offer to the people around you who are winning? When you realize that everyone deserves a chance to succeed—and others' hands do not have any bearing on your own—you can allow yourself to be happy for others and their successes. We all win if we play our cards right and see ourselves as the only competition in the game of life.

Remember that you're still in the game.

You can win with a bad hand. Bad luck, experiences, and cards don't have to discourage you. Use it all as your motivation. As long as you are breathing, you have a chance to claim victory. As long as you're motivated, you can change the game. Just don't give up!

#PlayForSomething

NBA player Brandon Jennings knows all too well that failure and loss can come in an instant. When he was eight years old, his father committed suicide, forcing Brandon to grow up fast. He turned to basketball for comfort and a way to deal with his frustrations. There are only a few hundred players in the NBA and over seven billion people in the world, but Brandon Jennings worked hard without focusing on the odds. Frankly, the odds didn't matter to him. As he put it, "Basketball was my way out. At a young age, I loved to play basketball. I wasn't into hanging out all the time."

Don't be afraid to give your all to something positive. Giving your all doesn't have to mean being the best—just making an honest effort will provide you with valuable experiences. Happy people don't have the best of everything, but they make the best of what they have. Walls will close in on you and people will bet against you. However, like Brandon Jennings, your reaction to the most difficult times will determine your outcome.

Growing up, I was no stranger to adversity. I had to be wheelchaired out of school a couple of times for painful kidney infections and ovarian cyst complications. I also had Bell's Palsy at one point in middle school and was temporarily paralyzed on the left side of my face while I struggled with balancing severe mood swings and hormones. Life!

I was always dealing with some ridiculous health issues that were beyond my control. However, no amount of complaining could change those things, so I had to adjust my way of thinking to deal with it. I could sulk or I could find strength. Knowing the options was my first step to overcoming it all.

I believe in a higher power that puts people through a series of tests. This belief gives me faith that everything wrong eventually becomes right, and it's taught me that patience is a virtue.

Every trial I've faced has made me stronger. I always prevail, which I credit to my ability to face every imaginary "life exam" head-on, knowing that I will succeed. Dealing with emergency surgeries as an adult was much easier because I had known pain in my past and never took feeling good and being healthy for granted. I look at my scars with a sense of gratitude: that's strength.

"ADVERSITY IS YOUR GIFT"

— Gary Vaynerchuk

Outlook Options

My good friend Alex struggles with pessimistic thoughts. Because things have often gone wrong in her life, in the past she found safety in not getting her hopes up so she could avoid potential disappointment. Alex thought, *If you give up hope on yourself and the people around you, then no matter the outcome, it won't make you feel more down.* She became *comfortable* being down and negative. Unfortunately, her constant sulking made her a drag to be around. It took Alex a long time to realize you can't produce better outcomes by sulking in fear and sorrow.

Pessimistic thoughts are very common with the youth I've met through Precious Dreams Foundation. In many cases, constant disappointment in their lives has trained them to believe bad news is always lurking around the corner. Negative perceptions and thoughts accompany almost all mental health disorders. The main disorder that results from this type of thinking is depression.

If you find yourself struggling to control unwanted thoughts or images, please know you are not alone. Depression is a treatable illness. Speak up and don't be afraid to tell a teacher or health professional if you need help. If you don't have a trusted adult in your life, call the National Youth Crisis Hotline at (800) 448-4663. One benefit to calling a toll-free hotline is that everything you say will remain anonymous and private. The hotline can also provide referrals to local treatment centers and shelters.

Depression is not something you can sleep away. It won't be cured by sitting in a dark room, drinking alcohol, or finding love in a hopeless place. Most teens suffering from depression hide their feelings behind excuses of stomachaches, headaches, and other physical pains.

What happens when you hide something? Does it disappear? No. It's still there, but covered. Just because other people can't see it doesn't mean it's going to get better. If you want to get rid of something, you need to do more than hide it away—you have to bring attention to it! The earlier you seek treatment, the faster you can experience relief, and the longer you have depression, the harder it becomes to overcome it.

How many days can you spend in the dark?

This is not a challenge or a rhetorical question but a thought exercise. Seriously, how long can you pull the blinds and close out a world of opportunity? How long can you choose darkness over light?

Did you know exposure to sunlight can help elevate your mood and energy? Research shows that the sun increases your serotonin levels which help to support feelings of happiness ☺ and calmness. Choosing darkness is a choice that encourages depression to stay. Don't encourage depression to stay!

Optimists see the glass as half full and are determined to achieve whatever they envision for themselves. Because of these positive tendencies, they often find success. I transformed from a pessimist to an optimist around the age of seventeen. My father had been suffering from depression for about ten years. I was going into my senior year of high school in Long Island and decided I was going to pursue my dreams, be happy, and go away (far away) to college. I worked hard during my junior year to improve my grades and get volunteer credits so I could get accepted to a great school and begin the positive and fulfilling life I imagined for myself. I could no longer take on the emotions of others and those who did not support me. I had to change my mindset for myself.

If you want to thrive in this life, find the motivation to want big things for yourself. For some people, that motivation comes from within, but for others it's not such a natural thing and assistance from a support group or therapy is needed. My father's depression was tough on everyone. I remember crying because I couldn't understand why he would act so cold toward me, but my mother helped me realize his actions had absolutely nothing to do with me. They were a reflection of his internal pain. Now, as an adult, I have a great relationship with my father. He's happy, he tells me he loves me, and he's proving to me that people change and grow at different speeds. It took him a long time to overcome depression, but I think time and consistent love from my stepmother inspired him to see more for himself.

Many times, people suffering from depression internalize their problems. They find it easier to deal with society by wearing a mask and hiding their pain or conflicted thoughts. Internalizing problems is a protective barrier that does not lead to success. Waiting for something or someone to make you happy won't work either. At the end of the day, depression is not something that goes away with good fortune or a happy relationship. It's a mental disorder that must be taken seriously and treated with care.

Pessimism is different from depression. If you have some measure of control over your thoughts, work each day to choose happiness. If you're waiting for bad things to happen, you won't be able to recognize when something good is staring you in the face.

Here's a tip: whenever something bad happens, instead of focusing on the bad, find one positive thing about the situation. Then move on.

For example: Having my parents split at age six was difficult, but my biggest gain from their situation was Yolanda Russell, my stepmom. Now, to be honest, I wasn't always open to the idea of having a stepparent, and I'm not going to lie and pretend I made her job easy. I definitely shouted the words, "You're not my mother!" once, maybe twice too many. But as I got older, I began to appreciate the void she filled in our home. She taught me how to cook and care for myself in ways only a woman could. I can't imagine what my life would've been like without her. Not to say my mother couldn't fulfill those things, but Yolanda was the best type of stepparent. I knew that she was young and unprepared for parenthood, but she chose to care for me when she didn't have to.

Life will continue to surprise you. It almost seems that no matter how hard you try, the tests will keep on coming, the characters in your life's movie will continue to change, and you'll eventually learn that giving up some control will make life easier. Take it one step at a time.

Ways you can advance over adversity:
- Create art, in any form.
- Master a skill.
- Read, read, read.
- Get up and get active.
- Make a plan—remember to continuously ask yourself, "Where am I going?" This question will help to keep you on a good path.
- Create a schedule that allocates time each day to do something you love. Call it your self-love hour. Doing things for yourself is a won-

derful thing. Adults have something called happy hour . . . a time where bars and restaurants offer discounted food and beverages, but teens need to find peace after a long day too. Do something that makes you feel safe and gives you room to breathe.

- Seek outside help if you need it. A support system and circle of optimistic friends can help boost your confidence and inspire feelings of gratitude.

Don't focus on winning, focus on *how*! It's a guaranteed way to make it to the finish line. After all, success stories are far more inspiring when they don't start with being dealt a lucky hand.

Chapter 16
Remedies and Takeaways:

- Never fold!

- You can win with a bad hand.

- It is your reaction to situations that determines the outcome.

- Internalizing your problems and hiding out is not a comfort mechanism. It's a temporary fix for an issue that still needs attention.

- No matter how weak you feel, hold tight to that small part of you that says, "I don't want to feel like this."

- Nobody deserves depression. If you think you're suffering from depression, seek help—not only for yourself but also for the people around you. Energy is transferable, and it's hard to watch your loved ones suffer.

CHAPTER 17

Giving Back Is Good for the Soul

"I realized that to 'give back' is to give what someone else has given you. When you were hungry, someone fed you, and so at some point if you volunteer to feed the homeless it's because you are giving back in a way that you've been helped."

—Octavia Yearwood,
author and former foster child

Octavia Yearwood, author of *How the Hell Did You Do That?*, found her purpose through teaching various forms of art therapy to children. Growing up, Octavia had to deal with a crackhead mother, transitioning through multiple foster homes, and feeling unloved. Life did not deal her a good hand, but she prioritized self-care and healing through travel and art exploration. Eventually, she found the confidence to share her story and wrote a book in hopes of inspiring other foster youth.

In the process of saving others, we can unintentionally save ourselves.

Sharing your story to inspire someone who may be battling the same issues is a big way to give back. Unfortunately, teens may not be open about their hardships because their peers may be cruel and judgmental when they haven't experienced or don't understand a situation.

You know the anxious feelings you wear when you're paranoid about a secret or something embarrassing being exposed? Those feelings not only haunt you but also take a toll on your mental and physical health. Opening up about your hardships initially feels like sitting down gently on a whoopie cushion. It may feel uncomfortable initially, but releasing your secrets or traumatic experiences will take away the power those experiences have over you and give you the ultimate release.

As teens, we often compare our lives to others' and sometimes find ourselves frustrated by what we don't have. You have to make the best of your current situation and focus on what you *do* have. You may feel like you don't have as much to give as someone else, but your gifts go beyond money and physical possessions. One easy way to recognize and focus on your gifts is to make a kind gesture for someone who is less fortunate.

Give Back
There is always someone less fortunate, and the world will never be short of volunteer opportunities. You can donate time by helping at an animal shelter, removing trash from the oceans, playing games with the elderly, or using your authentic skills to teach someone a subject, activity, or sport.

Use the internet to find a cause that you connect with. Are there any volunteer opportunities in your school or church? Colleges are looking for applicants who are committed to giving back and bettering their world. Volunteering can also make you eligible for local, state, and government scholarships.

What if you can only focus on the help *you* need?

Being afraid of losing what you already have is a common fear for youth who don't have much to begin with. They'll cling tight to the possessions or people in their lives and refuse to share out of fear of losing them. <u>Try focusing on gaining rather than retaining.</u> When you give or share, you receive even more in return. It won't happen every time, but that's how we learn where to give and in what ways we're valued and appreciated.

Help someone with their school work, do chores around the house, or find some other way to make someone else's life easier today. Giving back will deposit happiness coins into your mental bank account that no one will ever be able to withdraw. When considering ways to impact your community, try focusing on your authentic interests. Ask yourself how you want to be of service to the world. Volunteer in ways that make you feel useful.

Self-comforters understand the importance of doing good deeds for themselves as well. When you're happy or working on yourself, it'll feel easier to give back. Giving back gives you purpose and helps you figure out how you fit into society. You're one of 7 billion people in the world and YOU have the ability to make a difference.

#RewardsThroughGenerosity

With age, you learn to question societal problems and may begin to strategize about how to solve issues in your community or the world. Volunteering and taking action on the issues that matter to you will give you an insider's perspective. You'll be able to identify what's causing the issues, which will increase your ability to suggest effective change. Giving back also helps you learn the value of your time and work. Community service benefits all parties involved with both short-term and long-term results.

If you're compelled to give back in a new or unique way but can't find an organization or opportunity in your area, create the opportunity yourself. Starting a campaign, fundraising drive, or nonprofit takes a lot of passion and dedication, but it's not an impossible task. Create a mission and share your work with others. You'll be surprised how many people share your empathetic thoughts. It only takes one person to be the first to stand up and lead others toward positive change. If you want to start a club in your school or a nonprofit, do the research on how to get started and do it!

When I started Precious Dreams Foundation, I told myself we wouldn't stop until we provided comfort for youth all over America. I wanted PDF to grow to be a respected organization and a household name. I kept my expectations high and my work ethic even higher. Within six months of launching the organization, I received an email from *Glamour* magazine recognizing me as their 2013 Hero of the Year! One of my best friends submitted me for the award, and I was chosen out of hundreds of nominees. I was featured in a full-page spread, appeared in a commercial on primetime TV that highlighted PDF, and was given other recognition awards just for getting started and helping others. I hadn't even been in service for a year and my vision to help others on a grand scale was already coming to fruition.

Start small, and think big, but don't do it for the recognition. Don't do it hoping for something in return. Your efforts might not change the world, but they might improve the life of someone who will. It's not a written rule, it's just how the universe works.

Start a challenge. Do one good deed and then challenge your peers to do the same or something similar. Give it a name or a hashtag, post it, and encourage others to share. A little give-back inspiration and competition to better the world can be fulfilling and fun for all.

How much do you care about the following social issues or real world challenges on a scale from 1–5?

Immigration	1	2	3	4	5
Climate Change	1	2	3	4	5
Racial Equality	1	2	3	4	5
LGBTQ Equality and Civil Rights	1	2	3	4	5
Gun Control	1	2	3	4	5
Mental Health	1	2	3	4	5

Bullying	1	2	3	4	5
Mass Incarceration	1	2	3	4	5
Foster Care	1	2	3	4	5
Homelessness	1	2	3	4	5
Politics	1	2	3	4	5
Medical Related Issues	1	2	3	4	5
Self-Image Issues	1	2	3	4	5
Animal Rights	1	2	3	4	5
_____					
(Fill in the blank)	1	2	3	4	5

Do you understand the root causes of these issues? Do any of these things affect your daily life? In recognizing what affects you and your community, you'll find inspiration to become an agent for change. Start by learning what matters to you and then do research to find ways that you can advocate or help the issue. Use the internet and get started today. Make it a short or long-term project.

When you give back, the world says thank-you in ways you wouldn't believe.

Chapter 17
Remedies and Takeaways:

- What's wrong with sharing?

- You were given many gifts; it's time to pass them on to others.

- Share your time, resources, or personal story of overcoming adversity so you can lift up someone in need.

- Giving back gives you purpose.

- Show me an angry volunteer . . . not gonna happen. ¯_(ツ)_/¯

- When you give and share, you receive more. It's not a written rule, it's just how the universe works.

- Comfort involves being active to fix your own issues as well as the bigger picture.

CHAPTER 18

Holding on to Your Childhood

"Don't grow up too fast."
—some adult to every child at some point in their life

As a teen, I rolled my eyes at this quote more times than I can count. As an adult, I've learned to agree.

Remember when you were younger and played hide-and-seek? You ran off on your own, secretly desiring that the other player would never leave you alone for too long. The concept of the game and the idea of being found brought you joy and a sense of trust. It brought emotional satisfaction.

The inexperienced child always hid in the most obvious place or partially covered themselves while screaming, "Try to find me!" The more experienced hider would go for the darkest place, quiet their breaths, and challenge the seeker to really work. Not being found was the pits.

Although it means defeat, a part of the hider always hoped to hear the words, "I found you!"

Unfortunately, as people get older, they stop saying, "Try to find me." They just hide. The ways in which people hide are not always visible. They hide pieces of their personalities, their pasts, and their truths. They often have difficulty with trust. What happens as we grow that forces us to stop trusting that we'll be found? Shouldn't our greatest satisfaction come from living among people who find us every time? Shouldn't we surround ourselves with people who understand that when we say, "I'm fine," it might really translate to, "I'm having a bad day"? People who know exactly how to help. Why do adults continue to play hide-and-seek on their own complicated terms and not supply people with the instructions?

Real life hits you hard. You'll experience things and meet people that will tempt you to become jaded. With time, you'll begin to question everything, and the world won't seem like such an innocent place. Today, I challenge you to look around and absorb colors, sounds, clouds, and freedom for as long as you can. One day you'll look back and long for the fun.

Don't waste time missing out on the world!

Try to list five traits that you like about yourself and hope to hold on to in adulthood.

For example: My sensitivity. No matter how much people hurt me, I don't want to become a vengeful person.

1. _____

_____

2. _____

_____

3. _____

_____

4. _____

_____

5. _____

_____

#TeenTime

This is the time when fairy tales can still come true. There's time for wonder and play. Right now, there are no long-term consequences for feeling lost and unsure. You can explore every avenue, hobby, or subject you desire. You have teachers who can act as mentors and unlimited, free resources to help you with homework assignments. Until you turn eighteen, the law guarantees you support and shelter, even if your birth parents decide they can't raise you.

This is the time for figuring out what you like and what types of things and people you'd like to kick to the curb. Everything is possible. At this age, the world is your playground and your response to most mistakes can be forgiven with four simple words: "Sorry, I didn't know."

Growing up, I wrote music and put shows together in the house to entertain my stepmom. With a million things on her mind and life's responsibilities fraying her nerves, she always said the same thing to me: "Don't you have something better to do?!" But I didn't! Performing was how I enjoyed expressing myself. I was in the headspace where I just wanted to have fun. I couldn't understand why she wouldn't allow herself to appreciate that.

Teenagers are expected to carry themselves like mature adults but have limited freedom and benefits. When you can't get your way or do something "all the other kids" are already doing, it seems like you can't grow up fast enough. You want to exchange your freedom and play for work and responsibility just so you can stay out past curfew, have the latest technology, own some overpriced piece of clothing, or come and go as you please. Think about what that deal really looks like. This is usually one of those instances when you wish for something you don't really want, thinking the grass is greener on the other side. "Adulting" is serious business.

You get to be a teen for seven years and an adult for many more if you live to be one hundred and gray. Don't rush your life away. Enjoy yourself.

You are worried about the grass being greener on the other side and you can't even tell if that grass is real. People buy artificial turf every day!

Chapter 18
Remedies and Takeaways:

- The real world has no patience for innocent mistakes.

- Nobody should rush to take on adult responsibilities and bills. (You have your entire life for that.)

- Focus on your teen perks—yes, there are plenty.

- Look around and absorb colors, sounds, clouds, and freedom for as long as you can. One day you'll find yourself too busy to gaze out the window during the car rides.

- When you're an adult, people will look at you differently. They'll expect you to have all the answers (knowing they themselves don't know it all).

- How many adults use the term "playing" in their daily lives? You're not missing out on anything.

CHAPTER 19

Precious Dreams

"I was afraid to sleep at night. When I was in foster care, I remember I shared a bed with my two cousins in the basement and mice would jump over the bed at night."

—Darnell Thornton,
real estate agent and Precious Dreams Foundation
guest speaker

Patricia was thirteen years old and living in a two-bedroom apartment with three teenage boys, one cat, three dogs, a rabbit, and her seventy-year-old grandmother. The two options for Patricia were to sleep in the bed with her grandmother or sleep in the living room with her thirteen-year-old brother. With lights on, the front door opening and closing throughout the night, the TV blasting, and people sometimes sitting around her talking or arguing, Patricia attempted to go to bed each night and get proper rest for school. Some would say it's impossible to sleep in that type of environment, but when you've been moved around so much in your life, you eventually learn to sleep anywhere.

Darnell recalls a time when he was five years old and his foster family kept him and his two cousins locked in a basement at night. Mice would jump around the room and sometimes run across their bed. Bedtime was a scary time for him, but he was grateful to have his cousin there to make the situation more bearable. Eventually, Darnell was able to escape that horror story of a foster home when a family member stepped in to raise him.

Katy recalls the fear she had when she was fifteen and her father's best friend came to molest her at night. He waited until everyone was sound asleep and preyed on innocent Katy night after night. He manipulated her into believing that if she told anyone, he'd hurt her family and accuse her of lying. She felt powerless at night because no one had ever prepared her for what to do if someone sexually assaulted her. It felt wrong, but she was afraid to tell anyone. Katy suffered from insomnia and depression and hated bedtime. She didn't know that she had the power to stop this guy and protect herself at night. She never spoke up and could no longer dream.

These stories are sadly relatable to some of the youth we serve through Precious Dreams Foundation. However, whether your sleeping environment is safe or not, teens around the world are struggling to dream.

#SleepMatters

Many people dread the thought of climbing under the covers. Instead of being restful and relaxing, bedtime can be the time when your fears haunt you or outside noise seems to grow and take over your thoughts. I remember eavesdropping on arguments between my mom and dad at night. (I would actually sit up and put my ear to the wall.) After my parents split, I used music to self-soothe in bed to prevent my mind from wandering and focusing on things that were out of my control. Music was my escape.

Some teens find bedtime problematic because they'd prefer to sacrifice a good night's sleep for late-night fun or entertainment. A teen's internal clock, called their circadian rhythm, slightly shifts because of pubertal hormones, which cause melatonin (which helps you feel tired) to be produced later in the evening. You may not feel tired, but that doesn't mean you shouldn't try to rest. Developing a bedtime routine and getting a proper night's sleep is key for self-comfort.

How much sleep do you get each night?

According to the National Sleep Foundation in America, research from 2015 suggested these guidelines:
- **Children (age 6–13):** 9 to 11 hours
- **Teenagers (14–17):** 8 to 10 hours

- **Young adults (17–25):** 7 to 9 hours

Did you know your low energy and inability to concentrate or feel good could really be caused by lack of rest? Every major organ in your body suffers when you don't get enough sleep, and that includes your brain. Insufficient sleep has also been connected to aggression and bullying in children of all ages.

The symptoms of lack of sleep can even be confused for ADHD. Some common problems associated with sleep deprivation that are shared with ADHD symptoms include:
- mood swings
- difficulty concentrating on tasks
- aggressive behavior
- hyperactivity

Being deprived of sleep has negative effects on your physical and mental health and also impedes your ability to self-comfort. Precious Dreams Foundation's mission is to provide comfort and support for youth at bedtime. When you sleep good, you feel good.

No Phone Zone

The blue-and-white light of electronic screens should not get a companion pass to your bedroom. Phones and computers suppress the body's sleep chemicals; they lead to poor sleep quality and even insomnia. If you suffer from gadget addiction, you might even feel like your phone is your comfort item, but research has shown that it could be hurting you more than helping. Can the text messages, games, or websites wait for tomorrow? Just as you charge the battery on your phone, you must prioritize charging the body and the brain. Put your phone on airplane mode, leave it in another room, and practice taking nothing distracting to bed with you.

Rest in Peace

This saying should be used more often for those that are living. After all, we sleep for approximately one third of our lives. Quiet the noise and relax your mind at bedtime. You deserve to feel amazing tomorrow and the next day and the day after that. If you can't plan the way your day will pan out, you can at least give yourself the energy you need to face the obstacles.

Here is my personal recipe for a good night's rest:

- Use comfort items.
- Practice meditation or deep breathing.
- Close your eyes and count your blessings. This allows positive thoughts to take center stage.
- Take a bath or a shower. The hot water will make you feel tired as your body temperature drops and you'll be able to sleep in and skip this step in the morning.
- Put on clean and comfortable clothes or pajamas.
- Use a calming pillow mist (lavender is a good one).
- Listen to relaxing music, read a book, or write in a journal to unwind.

If this list isn't helpful, try writing yourself a letter of permission to do everything that's on your mind tomorrow. After all, you can't do much from bed but worry anyway.

Dear _____,

Tomorrow is a chance to _____

Tomorrow is a chance to _____

Tomorrow is a chance to _____

Tomorrow is a chance to _____

Tomorrow is a chance to _____

Then close the book and let it go. Tomorrow when you wake up, cross out your tomorrows and write the word "today" instead. Then you can act on your thoughts and get it done. :)

Be patient with yourself when sleep doesn't come easily. Quiet the mind, sleep in a safe space, and protect your Precious Dreams!

If you're someone seeking help for better sleep, try talking to a doctor, counselor, or sleep specialist for support.

Chapter 19
Remedies and Takeaways:

- Protect your sleep.

- Sleep enhances performance and brain activity.

- It's actually not cool to stay up all night. Taking care of your body is.

- Create a bedtime routine and environment that promote your best dreams.

- Your phone is not a healthy comfort item for bedtime.

- Quiet your mind. You can't solve your problems from bed. Tackle the unresolved problems in the morning.

FINAL CHAPTER

Just Have Fun!

"Have fun with life because it's all good, and even when it's not, it's still kind of good."

—Ryan Grant,
former NFL Super Bowl champion
and Precious Dreams Foundation board member

Fun?

I'm sure at some point you've said no to something only for someone else to chime in, "But come on, it's fun!" Who determines the fun? Does someone else's opinion on a political issue, sport, or subject sway your opinion? No, unless you're faking it for acceptance. What's good or fun is subjective, and *you* decide how to experience it.

Having fun means enjoying your time in your own way. It's that feeling when your insides smile and you're fully engaged in the moment. Fun does not deter you from the person you're working to create. It is not a distraction from the things you wish to do but a force that will boost your mood and help you along the way.

In 2006, Ryan Grant injured his left arm at the height of his career as a football player in the NFL. A night of celebrating with friends turned into an altercation, ending in a serious injury that sent Ryan to the ER. His injury caused damage to an artery, a tendon, and the ulnar nerve in his left arm, and he lost feeling in his left hand. He recalls that time in his life as a point when he felt full of fear and uncertainty. It was a tough lesson to learn—to recognize that his distractions from work unconsciously created a situation that could end his career.

"I took the game I love away from myself. So I was like, this could be your story: people will feel sorry for me or I could own it and prove to myself again that my philosophy of me creating my entire world is possible. So I changed my perspective and said, 'I have to find the positive in this.'"

Ryan went on to win a Super Bowl with the Green Bay Packers and didn't retire from the NFL until 2013. He faced countless obstacles, continuously added to his major injury list, and still persevered because of his thoughts. Even when things were bad, in his mind it was "still all good."

Today Ryan finds purpose in tackling issues in the community by providing mental health support to children and his peers. He is an active Precious Dreams Foundation board member and father of two, and he's currently building an awareness retreat in Tulum, Mexico, to help people create and heal. Ryan is someone who lived his dream as best as he could and is now fulfilling other goals by reaching out to inspire others to do the same. He shares his story because he realizes that if fun isn't aligned with your plan, it's simply a distraction.

Stay focused on your type of fun. Find friends to co-dream with and don't be afraid of change.

Live

Sometimes your thoughts are the biggest distraction from living in the moment. We find ourselves distracted by issues that are out of our control or worries that don't exist. Even in a world of chaos you must allow yourself to be present in your reality when it's good. Put energy and physical effort into this practice.

Protect your fun. Be selective of the spaces you occupy. Be prepared to express why something is good or bad for you to defend those decisions.

If you notice that someone's presence blocks your ability to let your guard down, go elsewhere. This is your life. These are your choices.

Every day is an opportunity to have a brand-new start, to rebuild a relationship, to work toward a plan for your future and to right your wrongs. Take advantage of your resources, master your talents, and grow to the best of your ability. Listen to your needs and build the life you deserve. It might be the hardest task, but it's the only way to live an enjoyable life.

With the right attitude, going through ups and downs will make you stronger. Even when living conditions, finances, and relationships don't develop the way you want them to, you can still have a positive outlook and treat your challenges as opportunities for growth. Even if nothing makes sense now, trust that it will eventually. Remember: if we didn't have bad days, we wouldn't be able to recognize good ones.

No really, live!
On average, Americans check their phones once every 12 minutes. How can you have fun when you can't commit yourself to a task or the people in front of you? Is your fun in places that other people are experiencing? Do you know how to entertain yourself? The people in the photos with the most likes are the ones having the fun, not those that are scrolling to like and like.

When you reflect back on what you did for the day, do you name all of the apps used, games played and text exchanged? If you do, you'll feel stagnant. Only when social media is being used to build a brand or run a business should you continuously invest most of your time there.

When is it over?
If a game has no rules and you've never played, how do you know when the fun is over?

You've never lived this life before, and you will never fully be prepared for what lies ahead. If you play in hopes of only seeing the final result you'll miss out on the fun that happens in the process. I named this Chapter "Final Chapter" instead of 20 so you'd know what it is. However, in life no one holds up a sign and says "Hey, guy, this is your last chapter . . ." Life just goes, and goes, until it ends. The biggest problem is that when facing adversity people give up on themselves, thinking it's the end when it's not.

You deserve to be happy and to make this your best life. Start manifesting your dreams and working toward the things you desire.

Mastering the ability to self-comfort is up to you. It doesn't come easy, but it's worth it. Don't you think you're worth it? Did you read this book because you thought you weren't? The purpose of self-comfort is to discover your inner strength and resilience. With this discovery, you can cope better and make wiser decisions.

Prioritizing self-comfort is not selfish. You should love yourself more than anything else in this world.

Go out there and love yourself harder, hold yourself tighter, and treat this life like a jump on the trampoline. You can go as high as you jump.

#KeepGoing

Mistakes are bound to happen, but trying is better than sitting on the sidelines. You are not defined by your mistakes or moments of weakness. You're just a teenager, at the beginning of a beautiful journey, growing the ability to self-regulate and empower yourself to be better each day. I wish you self-comfort and the ability to tap into your superpowers . . . because you're going to need it.

Revisit the chapters as necessary and pick me up when you need a pick-me-up. Self-comfort is never truly mastered, but the goal is to independently succeed and regulate your emotions in a healthy manner. You should want to win! You should want to heal, because when you're healing and addressing issues, life never feels like something you have to deal with!

Chapter 20
Remedies and Takeaways:

- Having fun shouldn't mean doing something that can harm your future.

- Self-comfort is the process of allowing yourself to have a good time.

- Are you having fun or are you on the phone?

- Before you know it, the times, the grades, the conflicts, and the seasons will all be behind you.

- Keep going!

- You should want to win—no one else can win for you.

Nothing is
promised in this life
(not even relationships); if
we don't learn to love, heal,
and cope without being
dependent on people or
things, we'll never survive.

About the Author

Nicole Russell is the cofounder and executive director of the Precious Dreams Foundation, where she has made a global impact on thousands of homeless and foster youth by teaching self-care and empowering young adults to harness their creative energies. She is a lead advocator for mental health, human rights, and the well-being of children. This New York native also inspires everyday people to become emotionally independent through her speaking engagements, private sessions, and seminars. Since the inception of Precious Dreams Foundation in 2012, Nicole's accolades include *GLAMOUR*'s Everyday Hero of the Year, a spot on *Observer*'s Top 20 Heroes Under 40, and Walmart's Community Playmaker Award, as well as a featured piece recognizing her efforts in *O, The Oprah Magazine*. When she's not giving back, Nicole enjoys playing golf, watching basketball, and writing music. Connect with her online at NicoleRussell.com and PreciousDreamsFoundation.org.